Favorite Psalms

Selected and expounded by

John Stott

MOODY PRESS

Scripture quotations in this
publication are from the *Holy Bible,
New International Version.*
Copyright © 1973, 1978, 1984 by
the International Bible Society.
Published in the U.K. by Hodder &
Stoughton.

Designed and created by
Three's Company
12 Flitcroft Street
London WC2H 8DJ

Worldwide co-edition organised and
produced by Angus Hudson Ltd
Greater London House
Hampstead Road
London NW1 7QX

Design: Peter M.Wyart MSIAD
Editor: Tim Dowley

Typesetting by Watermark

Printed in Great Britain by
Purnell Book Production Ltd
Paulton

British Commonwealth edition
published by
Word Publishing
Word (UK) Ltd
Milton Keynes
England

ISBN 0–85009–158–6

First published in the USA by
Moody Press
820 N. LaSalle Drive
Chicago, Il 60610
USA

ISBN 0–8024–4770–8

Moody Press, a ministry of the
Moody Bible Institute, is designed for
education, evangelization, and
edification. If we may assist you in
knowing more about Christ and the
Christian life, please write us without
obligation:
Moody Press, c/o MLM,
Chicago, Illinois 60610
USA

Contents

Preface   5

Psalm 1
The Way of the Righteous and the
Wicked   6

Psalm 8
What is a Human Being?   10

Psalm 15
An Uncorrupt Life   14

Psalm 16
Present Faith and Future Hope   18

Psalm 19
The Self-Revelation of God   21

Psalm 22
The Sufferings and Glory of Christ   26

Psalm 23
The Lord is My Shepherd   30

Psalm 24
Ascending the Hill of the Lord   33

Psalm 27
The Soul's Changing Moods   36

Psalm 29
The Voice of the Lord   40

Psalm 32
The Forgiveness and Guidance of God   44

Psalm 34
Boasting in God   47

Psalm 40
Out of the Horrible Pit   50

Psalms 42,43
The Causes and Cure of Spiritual
Depression   53

Psalm 46
Immanuel, God With Us   58

Psalm 51
Divine Mercy for the Penitent   62

Psalm 67
Saving Health to the Nations   66

Psalm 73
The Prosperity of the Wicked   70

Psalm 84
The Courts of the Lord   73

Psalm 90
Life's Transient Dream   77

Psalm 91
The Defence of the Most High   80

Psalm 95
An Invitation to Sing and to Hear   83

Psalm 98
Jehovah, the Savior-King   87

Psalm 100
The Lord is God and Good   91

Psalm 103
The Benefits of God's Grace   95

Psalm 104
The Works of God in Nature   98

Psalm 121
The Lord our Keeper   102

Psalm 122
The Peace of Jerusalem   104

Psalm 123
The Uplifted Eyes of Faith   106

Psalm 125
The Mountains round Mount Zion   108

Psalm 127
The Vanity of Unblessed Labor   110

Psalm 130
Out of the Depths   11

Psalm 131
A Child-like Humility   11

Psalm 133
Brothers Dwelling in Unity   11

Psalm 139
The All-seeing Eye of God   11

Psalm 145
In Praise of God's Kingdom   1

Psalm 150
The Final Doxology   1

Preface

It would be impossible to stop Christians singing. One of the sure signs of the fullness of the Holy Spirit is to "sing and make music in your heart to the Lord" (Ephesians 5:18,19). Especially when we come together to worship, our praises would be inconceivable without songs. So we say to one another, "Come, let us sing for joy to the Lord, let us shout aloud to the Rock of our Salvation" (Psalm 95:1).

In every generation new hymns have been written and published. Yet the oldest hymnbook of the church, the Psalter or Book of Psalms, has never lost its appeal.

Jesus Himself loved the Psalms. He often quoted them. He also applied some of them to Himself. He was David's son and lord (Psalm 110), He said, and the rejected stone which became the building's capstone (Psalm 118). He also saw Himself as experiencing the terrible sufferings of the innocent victim who is depicted, for example, in Psalms 22, 31, 41 and 59.

The reason why Christian people are drawn to the psalms is that they speak the universal language of the human soul. "The Book of Psalms," wrote Rowland E.Prothero in *The Psalms in Human Life* (1904) "contains the whole music of the heart of man." Whatever our spiritual mood may be, there is sure to be a psalm which reflects it – whether triumph or defeat, excitement or depression, joy or sorrow, praise or penitence, wonder or anger. Above all, the psalms declare the greatness of the living God as Creator, Sustainer, King, Lawgiver, Saviour, Father, Shepherd and Judge. As we come to know Him better through the Psalter, we fall down and worship Him.

A book called *The Canticles and Selected Psalms* was published in 1966 in Hodder and Stoughton's series of "Prayer Book Commentaries". It has long been out of print. I am therefore grateful to Tim Dowley for proposing the modernization and re-publication of some of the expositions in this beautifully illustrated edition.

John Stott
February 1988

Psalm 1

The Way of the Righteous and the Wicked

Jerome quoted the opinion of some that this first psalm is "the preface of the Holy Spirit" to the Psalter. It is certainly a very apt introduction. Two particular themes are found in it, which recur in many other psalms.

The first is the clear-cut distinction between *the righteous* and *the wicked*. The Bible as a whole, and specially the Wisdom Literature, divides humankind into these two absolute categories, and does not recognise a third. Psalms 32, 36 and 112 also compare and contrast the righteous and the wicked.

The second theme concerns the present fortunes and the ultimate destinies of human beings. The first and last words of Psalm 1 indicate the alternatives. *Blessed* is the righteous person who delights in God's law; the ungodly, on the other hand, will *perish*. This process of "blessing" and "cursing," as Jeremiah called it when he perhaps elaborated this psalm (see Jeremiah 17:5-8), is already discernible in this life.

The West Wall, or Wailing Wall, Jerusalem, which gets its name from the lamentation of the Jews for the destruction of the Temple. It was the only part of the Temple that was almost always accessible to them.

In handling these two themes the author of Psalm 1 is only anticipating what Jesus Himself was to teach, that men and women are either on the broad road that leads to destruction or on the narrow way that leads to life (Matthew 7:13, 14).

The righteous will prosper (verses 1-4)

The righteous person is described first negatively, then positively. He or she *does not walk in the counsel of the wicked or stand in the way of sinners or sit in the seat of mockers.* These expressions have been carefully composed in a triple set of parallels: "walk, stand, sit," "counsel, way, seat," and "wicked, sinners, mockers." Moreover, a downward progression is implied. The godly do not model their conduct on the

Blessed is the man
who does not walk in the counsel of
the wicked
or stand in the way of sinners
or sit in the seat of mockers.

But his delight is in the law of the LORD,
and on his law he meditates day and
night.

³He is like a tree planted by streams of
water,
which yields its fruit in season
and whose leaf does not wither.
Whatever he does prospers.

⁴Not so the wicked!
They are like the chaff
that the wind blows away.

⁵Therefore the wicked will not stand in
the judgment,
nor sinners in the assembly of the
righteous.

⁶For the LORD watches over the way of
the righteous,
but the way of the wicked will perish.

advice of bad people. Further, the godly do not linger in the company of persistent evildoers; still less remain permanently among the cynical who openly scoff at God.

Instead of taking the lead from such people, the godly make *the law of the LORD* their rule (verse 2). This *law (Torah)* refers not just to the Ten Commandments, or even all the rules and regulations of the law of Moses, but to all God's revelation as the guide of life, which, although given through Moses and the prophets, is yet *the law of the LORD,* a phrase virtually equivalent to "the word of God".

The law of the Lord is the righteous person's *delight.* This an indication of new birth, for "...the sinful mind is hostile to God. It does not submit to God's law, nor can it do so" (Romans 8:7). As a result of the inward, regenerating work of the Holy Spirit, however, the godly find that they love the law of God simply because it conveys to them the will of their God. They do not rebel against its exacting demands; their whole being approves and endorses it (see Psalms 19; 40:8; 112:1 119). Delighting in it, the godly will *meditate* in it, or pore over it, constantly, day and night.

It is believed that this was the favorite text of Jerome, the author of the old Latin version of the Bible. He certainly exemplified it in his life, relentlessly pursuing his study of the Scriptures first in the desert, and then for nearly thirty-five years in his grotto near the traditional scene of the Nativity in Bethlehem. Indeed, all Christians know something of the psalmist's experience. To them daily meditation in the Bible is an unending delight.

This, then, is the characteristic of the righteous. For guidance regarding daily conduct they look not to public opinion, the unreliable fashions of the godless world, but to the revealed Word of God, in which they delight and meditate. As a result they are *like a tree planted by streams of water* (verse 3).

The metaphor is a common one in the Bible. Whatever kind of tree is in mind, it clearly enjoys the secret of perennial health and vigour, its fruit ripening in its season, and its leaf not withering even under the heat of the sun; for as the tree draws constant nourishment from the water through its roots, so through daily meditation in the law of the Lord the righteous refresh and replenish their soul in God. Such a tree is firmly *planted;* such people, like Joshua, prosper in whatever they do.

The ungodly will perish (verses 5, 6)
Not so the wicked! Their present condition and future destiny are entirely different. Instead of being like a fruitful tree, they are like dry and useless chaff. Instead of being planted by the waterside, they are driven by the wind.

Again, the metaphor was a familiar one in Bible days and

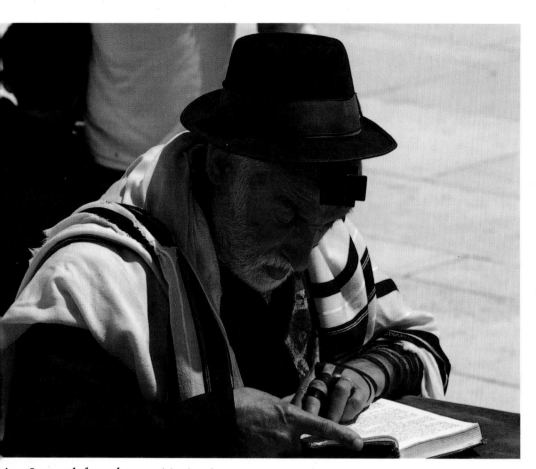

Bible lands (compare Psalm 35:5; Isaiah 17:13; Matthew 3:12). The threshing floor was usually a hard, flat surface situated on a hill, well exposed to the wind. The wheat was lifted by large winnowing fans or shovels and thrown into the air, so that the precious grain would drop down and be garnered, while the light husks of the chaff would be scattered to the four winds.

The wicked *are like chaff* in two senses. They are desiccated and unprofitable in themselves; and they are easily blown away by the judgment of God. The basic idea behind the Hebrew word for *the wicked* appears to be one of "restlessness" (compare Isaiah 57:20,21). The tree is planted firmly; but the chaff is unstable. When God begins to sift them in His present activity of judgment, and specially when the final day of judgment comes, they will not stand. Not even now can they stand *in the assembly of the righteous,* for they do not belong to the godly remnant of His people.

Verse 6 is a general conclusion to the whole psalm, distinguishing between *the way of the righteous* and *the way of the wicked.* We are told that the Lord *watches over the way of the righteous*; whereas *the way of the wicked will perish.*

Psalm 8

What is a Human Being?

Twilight in the hills. "O LORD, our Lord, how majestic is your name in all the earth! You have set your glory in the heavens."

"This short, exquisite lyric," as it was called by C.S.Lewis begins and ends with the refrain: *O LORD, our Lord, how majestic is your name in all the earth.* Here is a recognition of the majesty of God's name, or nature, which His works reveal in both earth and heaven. The enemies of God, blinded by their proud rebellion, do not see His glory; but they are confounded by *children and infants.* Jesus quoted these words when the children acclaimed Him in the Temple with their hosannas, while the chief priests and scribes indignantly objected (Matthew 21:15,16). God is still glorified in the simple faith of children and in the childlike humility of Christian believers (see Matthew 11:25,26; 1 Corinthians 1:26-29).

¹O LORD, our Lord,
 how majestic is your name in all the
  earth!

You have set your glory
 above the heavens.
²From the lips of children and infants
 you have ordained praise
because of your enemies,
 to silence the foe and the avenger.

³When I consider your heavens,
 the work of your fingers,
the moon and the stars,
 which you have set in place,
⁴what is man that you are mindful of him,
 the son of man that you care for him?

What particularly evokes the wondering worship of the psalmist is God's condescension toward human beings (verses 3,4) and the position of dominion which He has granted to them on earth (verses 5-8). Seen in relation to each other, these two truths enable us to have a balanced judgment of human-kind and to give a proper answer to the psalmist's rhetorical question, *What is man?* (verse 4), that is, What does it mean to be a human being?

The littleness of human beings (verses 3,4)

The question was prompted by a consideration of the night sky. If David was the author of this psalm, there can be little doubt that he was referring to the experience of his youth. In his shepherd days, tending his father's flock in the hills near Bethlehem, he often slept under the stars. Lying on his back, he would survey the fathomless immensity above him, seeking to penetrate the clear depths of the eastern sky. He recognised that the heavens, with the moon and the stars, were the work

---

ı made him a little lower than the
      heavenly beings
ınd crowned him with glory and
      honour.

6You made him ruler over the works of
      your hands;
   you put everything under his feet:
7all flocks and herds,
      and beasts of the field,

8the birds of the air,
      and fish of the sea,
   all that swim the paths of the seas.

9O LORD, our Lord,
      how majestic is your name in all the
         earth!

of God's fingers (verse 3), and as he contemplated their great ness and mystery, he cried out: *What is man that you are mindful of him, and the son of man that you care for him?* (verse 4).

If this was David's reaction, nearly three thousand years ago, how much more should it be ours who live in days of astro-physics and the conquest of space? As we consider the orbiting planets of our solar system, so infinitesimally small in comparison with countless galaxies millions of light years distant, it may seem to us incredible that the great God of the universe should take any note of us at all, let alone *care for* us. Yet He does; and Jesus assured us that even the hairs of our head are all numbered.

The greatness of human beings (verses 5-8)

The psalmist moves from the littleness of a human being, in comparison with the vastness of the universe, to the greatness which God has given him on earth: *You made him a little lower than the heavenly beings and crowned him with glory and honor. You made him ruler over the works of your hands* (verses 5,6).

Our position of only slight inferiority to the heavenly beings or even to God Himself, is supremely seen in our *rule*. God has invested human beings with royal sovereignty, crowning us with glory and honor (verse 5) and delegating to us the control of His works. It is even stated that God has put *everything under his* (man's) *feet.*

The psalmist is referring primarily to the animal creation, beasts both domesticated and wild, *the birds of the air, and the fish of the sea,* and all other creatures inhabiting the depths of the ocean (verses 7,8). This is not poetic fiction. As the universe yields more and more of its secrets to scientific research, so our dominion increases. Yet even now humankind is not, in fact, lord of creation, with *everything* under our feet, as is recognised in the three New Testament quotations of these verses.

According to Hebrews 2:5 and the following verses: "... at present we do not see everything subject to him." It is immediately added, however: "But we see Jesus, who was made a little lower than the angels, now crowned with glory and honour." Humankind has sinned and fallen, and consequently has lost some of the dominion which God had given us; but in Jesus, the second Adam, this dominion has been restored. It is in Him rather than in us that humankind's dominion is exhibited. By His death He even destroyed the devil and delivered his slaves (verses 14, 15). He has now been "crowned", and exalted to God's right hand.

Although the Psalm's description of humankind's dominion is true rather of the man Christ Jesus than of us, it applies to us also if we have come by faith to share in His exaltation. The apostle Paul wrote that the exceeding greatness of God's power, which exalted Jesus and "put everything under his feet," is available to us who believe (Ephesians 1:19-22). Indeed, we have experienced it, for it has raised us from the death of sin, exalted us with Christ and made us sit with Him in the heavenly places, where we are partakers of his victory and dominion (Ephesians 2:5,6).

Even this is not the end. Although Christ is exalted far above all rule and authority, and all things are potentially under His feet, not all His enemies have yet conceded their defeat or surrendered to Him. Only when He appears in glory and the dead rise, will He destroy "all dominion, authority and power. For he must reign until he has put all his enemies under his feet. The last enemy to be destroyed is death. For He 'has put every thing under his feet'" (1 Corinthians 15:24-26).

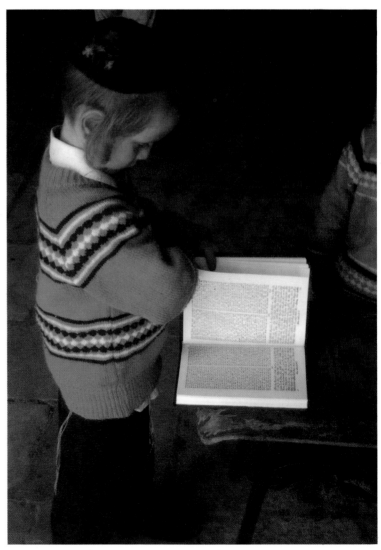

oung Jewish boy reads
Scriptures at the
agogue at the Wailing
ll, Jerusalem. The
agogue is near the
called Wilson Arch,
e an entrance to the
nple.

Psalm 15

An Uncorrupt Life

Psalm 15 is concerned with the conditions on which a man or
woman may dwell with God. It is especially noteworthy
because it unites religion and morality in an indissoluble
partnership. It opens with a question, continues with an answer to the question posed, and concludes with a grand assertion which goes beyond the terms of the original question.

The question (verse 1)
*Lord, who may dwell in your sanctuary? Who may live on
your holy hill?* God's *holy hill* was of course Jerusalem and his
sanctuary probably the tent which housed the ark before Solomon built the Temple. Indeed, it has generally been thought
that this psalm, like Psalm 24, refers to the occasion, described
in 2 Samuel 6:12-19 and 1 Chronicles 15 and 16, when David
brought the ark from the house of Obed-edom on to Mount
Zion, "the city of David," and placed it in the tent which he
had pitched for it. In this case, the psalm outlines the moral
challenge which God's presence in their midst brought to the
inhabitants of Jerusalem.

But the psalm has a wider application than this. It inquires
into the terms on which any human being may dwell in God'

> ¹LORD, who may dwell in your
>   sanctuary?
>   Who may live on your holy hill?
>
> ²He whose walk is blameless
>   and who does what is righteous,
>   who speaks the truth from his heart
> ³   and has no slander on his tongue,
>   who does his neighbour no wrong
>   and casts no slur on his fellow man,
> ⁴who despises a vile man
>   but honours those who fear the
>   LORD,
>   who keeps his oath
>   even when it hurts,
> ⁵who lends his money without usury
>   and does not accept a bribe against
>   the innocent.
>
> He who does these things
>   will never be shaken.

An Arab merchant in the vegetable market in Bethlehem.

presence, either in this life or in the life to come. The psalm is clear that Jehovah is a holy God and that sinners separa themselves from God by their sin. "You are not a God w takes pleasure in evil; with you the wicked cannot dwel (Psalm 5:4). Who, then, may dwell with God?

The answer (verses 2-6)
The psalmist now answers his own question and describes t kind of person who may draw near to God. He paints attractive picture. Indeed, no one has perfectly fulfilled tl ideal except the man Christ Jesus. Jesus Christ alone h

entered the presence of God in heaven in virtue of His own merit; for us access to God is possible only through Christ.

But, having been brought near to God by Christ, we can enjoy continuing fellowship with Him only if by His grace we lead the kind of holy life which this psalm depicts. It is a social holiness. That is, it concerns entirely our duty to our neighbor, since we cannot have a right relationship with God without a right relationship with human beings. We cannot expect to dwell in God's presence if we are not seeking our neighbor's good.

So the people who may enjoy God's company are described as *blameless* (verse 2). They are people of such complete integrity of character that they both do what is right and speak what is true. Further, the truth they speak is from their *heart,* for they always mean what they say. They are thus consistent in thought, word, and deed.

This general and positive statement is now illustrated by particular and largely negative examples. Indeed, it is against the background of these negatives that the positive excellence of good people stands out in shining relief.

First, they do not harm their neighbors by anything they say or do (verse 3). They neither slander them, nor wrong them, nor cast slurs against them. This last expression probably means either that they do not repeat gossip about their neighbors, or that they do not take unfair advantage of them when they are overtaken by adversity. Secondly, they are discerning in their assessment of others (verse 4). They are not afraid to express disapproval of worthless people. Thirdly, they are faithful to their promises, even when it is to their own inconvenience or disadvantage. They are people of their word (verse 5). Fourthly, they never exploit the poor or oppress the innocent (verse 6).

More precisely, they do not lend money on usury or accept bribes. We are introduced here to familiar figures in the Old Testament – the extortionate moneylender and the unjust magistrate who perverts justice for a bribe. Both practices were forbidden by the law (Exodus 22:25; Leviticus 25:35-38 and Exodus 23:6-8; Deuteronomy 16:19; 27:25) and denounced by the prophets (see, for example, Ezekiel 22:12).

The assertion (verse 7)

The psalmist has asked who shall dwell in God's presence, and has answered his own question by portraying a person who loves his or her neighbor. But he does not stop there. Such people, he concludes, will not only abide in God's sanctuary; they *will never be shaken.* On the contrary, they will remain firm and secure throughout all the vicissitudes of this life, and on the day of judgment.

Psalm 16

Present Faith and Future Hope

Although this psalm opens with a prayer (*Keep me safe, God*), it is in reality a believer's testimony regarding both h[is] present faith and his future hope. Having taken refuge in G[od] (verse 1), he has found in Him his greatest good (verses 2,6,[ ]) and is convinced that even death cannot rob him of that tr[ue] life which consists of fellowship with God (verses 11,12[ ]) These final verses were applied to the resurrection of Jes[us] Christ by Peter on the day of Pentecost and by Paul in t[he] synagogue of Antioch in Pisidia (Acts 2:24-31; 13:34-37).

Present faith (verses 1-6)

What it means to put one's trust in God, or to *take refu[ge]* (verse 1) in Him, is explained in verse 2 (compare Psal[m] 73:24). The believer has turned from the pleasures of sin a[nd] the vanities of the world to seek and find his good in Go[d.] Delighting in God, he delights also in the godly, the *sain[ts]* (verse 3).

In the ungodly, however, who have exchanged the true a[nd] living God for *other gods* (verse 4), the believer takes [no] delight. He knows that they will have great trouble – their *so[r]rows... will increase*. He affirms with resolve that he w[ill] neither offer their idolatrous libations of blood nor even me[n]tion the names of their false deities (verse 5). To do so wou[ld] be incompatible with his wholehearted devotion to the Lor[d] of whom he now writes in the most exalted terms (verses 5,6[)]

¹Keep me safe, O God,
  for in you I take refuge.

²I said to the LORD, "You are my Lord;
  apart from you I have no good thing."
³As for the saints who are in the land,
  they are the glorious ones in whom
  is all my delight.
⁴The sorrows of those will increase
  who run after other gods.
I will not pour out their libations of blood
  or take up their names on my lips.

⁵LORD, you have assigned me my
  portion and my cup;
you have made my lot secure.
⁶The boundary lines have fallen for me
  in pleasant places;
surely I have a delightful inheritance.

⁷I praise the LORD, who counsels me;
  even at night my heart instructs me.
⁸I have set the LORD always before me.
  Because he is at my right hand,
  I shall not be shaken.

⁹Therefore my heart is glad and my
  tongue rejoices;
my body also will rest secure,
¹⁰because you will not abandon me to
  the grave,
  nor will you let your Holy One see
  decay.
¹¹You have made known to me the path
  of life;
you will fill me with joy in your
  presence,
with eternal pleasures at your right
  hand.

The Garden Tomb, East Jerusalem. Though it is most unlikely that Jesus was buried and arose from this tomb, many visitors find this garden a haven of tranquility.

The Lord has assigned him his *portion* (alluding probably to a portion of food rather than of land) and his *cup*, thus both satisfying his hunger and quenching his thirst. Further, he has found God to be a *delightful inheritance*, just like the Levitical priests, who were given no inheritance in Canaan because their inheritance was the Lord (see, for example, Numbers 18:20).

Future hope (verses 7-11)

David, who according to the apostles Peter and Paul was the author of this psalm, now breaks out into thanksgiving (verse 7) that the Lord has given him *counsel* and that *at night* his *heart instructs* him. What this divine instruction is which he has received he does not make clear. It seems best to refer it to the remaining verses of the psalm.

God draws near to David and speaks to him; his own heart teaches him while in the stillness of the night he meditates on his intimate fellowship with God. He learns to draw from his experience this mighty deduction: that because God is ever before him and beside him (verse 8), *I shall not be shaken.* other words, the blessings of his communion with God cann be limited to his satisfaction only; they include his securi also. His present faith brings a future hope.

David now rejoices in heart and soul because he is convinc that his body also may *rest secure* (verse 9). He goes on elaborate his new assurance in direct speech to God (vers 11,12).

Three levels of interpretation are possible in these verses, of which are true. Literally they express the writer's confiden that he will not die, that his soul will not be delivered *to t grave* – the translation of the Hebrew *sheol*, the abode of t dead. Nor will his body *see decay*. We do not know the histc ical circumstances in which the psalm was written, but it m possibly express the confidence which sustained David duri his months as an outlaw, that he would not be delivered in the hand of Saul.

The implication of these verses goes further than this, ho ever. The corollary to deliverance from death is treading t *path of life*; and this life is seen to be no mere physical surviv but the enjoyment of God's presence bringing *joy* and *eterr pleasures.* It is in fact what the New Testament calls "eterr life," communion with God, which physical death cann interrupt. It is unlikely that David understood fully what was writing, since life and immortality were only clea: revealed by Jesus Christ (2 Timothy 1:10); yet his words fi their true fulfillment only in the consummation of eternal l beyond the grave.

When Peter applied these verses to the resurrection of Jesu he went so far as to say that David cannot have been referri primarily to himself, since he died and was buried. He went c "But he was a prophet and knew that God had promised h on oath that he would place one of his descendants on I throne. Seeing what was ahead, he spoke of the resurrection the Christ, that he was not abandoned to the grave, nor did I body see decay" (Acts 2:30,31).

We must be careful not to make Peter say more than he act ally did say. He himself in his first letter (1 Peter 1:10-1 explained that the prophets did not fully understand to wh the Spirit of Christ within them was referring when predicti Christ's sufferings and subsequent glory. We need not the fore assert that David was making a deliberate and conscic prophecy of the resurrection of Jesus which was fully intelli ble to himself. It is enough to say that, caught up by the Sp of prophecy, he was led to write words about the conquest death and the fulness of life and joy in the presence of Gc which would be finally fulfilled not in his own experience b in that of his illustrious descendant.

Psalm 19

The Self-Revelation of God

According to C.S.Lewis, this is "the greatest poem in the Psalter and one of the greatest lyrics in the world." From the Christian point of view it contains the clearest summary of the doctrine of revelation to be found in the Old Testament, namely that God has made Himself known to all humankind as Creator (verses 1-6), to Israel as Lawgiver (verses 7-10), and to the individual as Redeemer (verses 11-14).

General revelation (verses 1-6)

Human beings cannot plead ignorance of God, since He never ceases to give a revelation of Himself, which is called "general" because it is made to all people everywhere. As the apostle Paul put it, he has not "left himself without testimony" (Acts 14:17; compare Acts 17:22-28 and Romans 1:20).

This witness is in nature, especially here *the heavens*, which *declare the glory of God* because they are *the work of his hands* (verse 1). Even more today, through the cosmology of modern astrophysics, the heavens, "their vastness, splendor, order and mystery" as one commentator puts it, reveal God's glory and greatness.

God's witness to Himself through the heavens has three characteristics. First, it is continuous. *Day after day... night after night* (verse 2) the testimony is given without intermission. Secondly, it is abundant. The verb in verse 2 is expressive: *they* (the heavens) *pour forth speech*. Thirdly it is universal. Although *there is no speech or language* (verse 3), yet by sight rather than sound their message penetrates to the end of the world (verse 4). Paul even applies this last verse to the worldwide spread of the gospel (Romans 10:18).

Of this universal witness to God by the heavens, the sun is a particular example. In dramatic imagery, which is not of course intended to be taken literally, the psalmist likens the sunrise to the emergence of a bridegroom from his chamber, and its daily course across the sky to the running of an athlete, so that *nothing is hidden from its heat* (verse 6).

Special revelation (verses 7-10)

Abruptly and without warning the subject changes from God's general and natural revelation through creation to His special and supernatural revelation through *torah*, "the law," which

Sunset over the Sea of
Galilee. "The heavens
declare the glory of God;
the skies proclaim the
work of his hands."

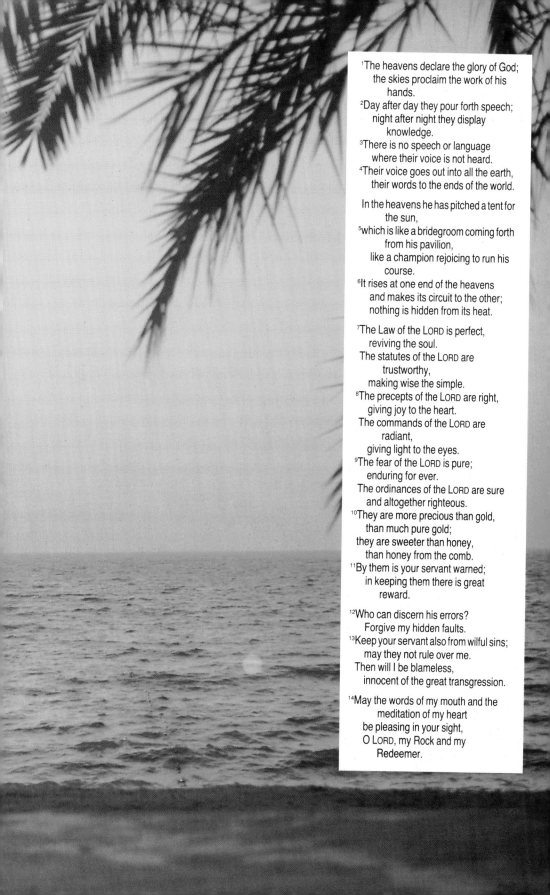

¹The heavens declare the glory of God;
   the skies proclaim the work of his
      hands.
²Day after day they pour forth speech;
   night after night they display
      knowledge.
³There is no speech or language
   where their voice is not heard.
⁴Their voice goes out into all the earth,
   their words to the ends of the world.

In the heavens he has pitched a tent for
   the sun,
⁵which is like a bridegroom coming forth
      from his pavilion,
   like a champion rejoicing to run his
      course.
⁶It rises at one end of the heavens
   and makes its circuit to the other;
   nothing is hidden from its heat.

⁷The Law of the LORD is perfect,
   reviving the soul.
The statutes of the LORD are
      trustworthy,
   making wise the simple.
⁸The precepts of the LORD are right,
   giving joy to the heart.
The commands of the LORD are
      radiant,
   giving light to the eyes.
⁹The fear of the LORD is pure;
   enduring for ever.
The ordinances of the LORD are sure
   and altogether righteous.
¹⁰They are more precious than gold,
   than much pure gold;
they are sweeter than honey,
   than honey from the comb.
¹¹By them is your servant warned;
   in keeping them there is great
      reward.

¹²Who can discern his errors?
   Forgive my hidden faults.
¹³Keep your servant also from wilful sins;
   may they not rule over me.
Then will I be blameless,
   innocent of the great transgression.

¹⁴May the words of my mouth and the
      meditation of my heart
   be pleasing in your sight,
   O LORD, my Rock and my
      Redeemer.

refers not merely to the law of Moses but to all Old Testame[nt] Scripture. The transition, though abrupt, is not arbitrary. Th[e] heavens and the law both make God known. Furthe[r] C.S.Lewis may be right to detect a link in the reference to t[he] all-pervasive heat of the sun, so that "the searching and clean[s]ing sun becomes an image of the searching and cleansing law."

With the change of subject comes a significant change in t[he] divine name. The One who reveals Himself in nature to [all] people is *God*, Hebrew *El* (verse 1), the God of creation; but [it] is the LORD Yahweh (seven times in the second half of t[he] psalm), the God of the covenant, who has revealed Hims[elf] through His law to His covenant people Israel. It is a revelati[on] not now of His glory but of His will, and its excellencies are s[et] forth in perfect Hebrew parallelism (verses 7-9).

The symmetry of these verses is so precise that each begi[ns] with a different aspect of God's will, and goes on to descri[be] both what it is and what it does. Thus, *the law*, or divi[ne] instruction, is *perfect*, bearing witness to God's nature expre[s]sed in His will, and consists of particular *statutes, precep[ts]* and *commands*. Its perfection is seen in the fact that its injun[c]tions are *trustworthy, right, radiant, pure, sure and altogeth[er] righteous*. It is also called *the fear of the LORD* (verse 9) becau[se] the great end of all revelation is to inspire a humble and reve[r]rent worship of God. This disclosure of God's will is said to [be] *pure*.

But the psalmist does not merely contemplate the law of t[he] Lord as it is in itself; he also unfolds its beneficial effects, *rev[iv]ing the soul*, rejoicing the heart and, above all, *making w[ise]* (verse 7) and *giving light* (verse 8) to those who are humb[le] enough, or (as our Lord was later to teach) childlike enough, [to] receive it. The inherent qualities and health-giving results [of] God's law make it *more precious than gold... sweeter... th[an] honey from the comb* (verse 10).

It may be surprising to us that the writer did not find Go[d's] law a burden to him; we may feel with C.S.Lewis that his refe[r]ence to its sweetness is at first sight "very mysterious," ev[en] "utterly bewildering." The explanation is not just that its co[m]mandments were right, nor that its promises were sure, b[ut] that it was the revelation of God, the special means which [He] had chosen to make Himself known to His people Israel.

Personal revelation (verses 11-14)
With verse 11 the psalmist for the first time mentions himse[lf.] He has been describing how *all the earth* (verse 4) m[ay] apprehend God's glory from nature, and how *the simple* (ver[se] 7) may derive wisdom from God's law. But he concludes [his] psalm by disclosing his personal spiritual aspirations as Go[d's] *servant* (verses 11,13).

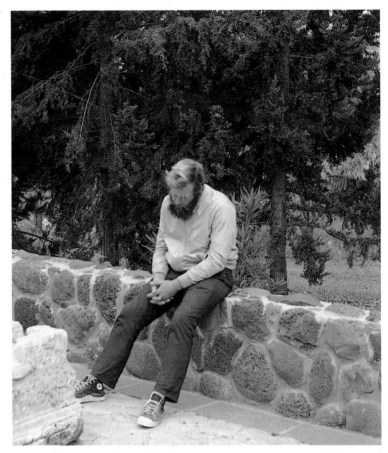

A pilgrim to the Holy Land. "May the words of my mouth and the meditation of my heart be pleasing in your sight, O LORD, my Rock and my Redeemer."

He has himself found wholesome warning in God's law and knows that conformity to it brings great reward (verse 11). He seems to have discovered in his own experience the dual purpose of the divine law, namely to reveal sin (Romans 3:20) and to promote holiness. This leads him both to pray for cleansing from the *hidden faults* (verse 12) which he has committed, and for deliverance from *wilful sins* (verse 13) which he longs to avoid, so that he is not mastered by them but is kept *innocent of great transgression.* The psalmist is not referring here to any one particularly grievous sin, or even the blasphemy against the Holy Spirit (as poor John Bunyan thought), but to all deliberate wrongdoing, sins committed "defiantly" (Numbers 15:30,31).

The psalm ends with a prayer which is frequently echoed by Christian ministers before they preach. In it the writer goes beyond his plea for deliverance, to a positive and very personal desire that all his words, and even his thoughts, shall be *pleasing* in the sight of God, whom he now declares to be both his *Rock* ("strength") and his *Redeemer.* Redemption is in itself negative deliverance from sin; it needs to be completed by a life that is pleasing to God (see Titus 2:14).

Psalm 22

The Sufferings and Glory of Christ

This is the first of a number of so-called "passion psalms" in the Psalter, which describe the suffering and persecution of an innocent victim in terms reminiscent of the Suffering Servant of the Lord in the second part of Isaiah. Although some commentators have suggested that the godly sufferer is more ideal than real, representing perhaps the Israelite nation when exiled among the heathen, the narrative of his afflictions is so vivid in its details that it undoubtedly depicts a true and literal experience.

¹My God, my God, why have you forsaken me?
Why are you so far from saving me, so far from the words of my groaning?
²O my God, I cry out by day, but you do not answer,
by night, and am not silent.

³Yet you are enthroned as the Holy One; you are the praise of Israel.
⁴In you our fathers put their trust; they trusted you and you delivered them.
⁵They cried to you and were saved; in you they trusted and were not disappointed.

⁶But I am a worm and not a man, scorned by men and despised by people.
⁷All who see me mock me; they hurl insults, shaking their heads:
⁸"He trusts in the LORD; let the LORD rescue him.
Let him deliver him, since he delights in him."

⁹Yet you brought me out of the womb; you made me trust in you
even at my mother's breast.
¹⁰From birth I was cast upon you; from my mother's womb you have been my God.
¹¹Do not be far from me, for trouble is near
and there is no-one to help.

¹²Many bulls surround me; strong bulls of Bashan encircle me.
¹³Roaring lions tearing their prey open their mouths wide against me.
¹⁴I am poured out like water, and all my bones are out of joint.
My heart has turned to wax; it has melted away within me.
¹⁵My strength is dried up like a potsherd, and my tongue sticks to the roof of my mouth;
you lay me in the dust of death.
¹⁶Dogs have surrounded me; a band of evil men has encircled me,
they have pierced my hands and feet.
¹⁷I can count all my bones; people stare and gloat over me.
¹⁸They divide my garments among them and cast lots for my clothing.

¹⁹But you, O LORD, be not far off; O my Strength, come quickly to help me.
²⁰Deliver my life from the sword, my precious life from the power of the dogs.
²¹Rescue me from the mouth of the lions; save me from the horns of wild oxen.

²²I will declare your name to my brothers; in the congregation I will praise you.
²³You who fear the LORD, praise him!
All you descendants of Jacob, honour him!
Revere him, all you descendants of Israel!

²⁴For he has not despised or disdained the suffering of the afflicted one;
he has not hidden his face from him but has listened to his cry for help.

²⁵From you comes my praise in the great assembly;
before those who fear you, will I fulfil my vows.
²⁶The poor will eat and be satisfied; they who seek the LORD will praise him –
may your hearts live for ever!
²⁷All the ends of the earth will remember and turn to the LORD,
and all the families of the nations will bow down before him,
²⁸for dominion belongs to the LORD, and he rules over nations.

²⁹All the rich of the earth will feast and worship;
all who go down to the dust will kneel before him –
those who cannot keep themselves alive.
³⁰Posterity will serve him; future generations will be told about the LORD.
³¹They will proclaim his righteousness to a people yet unborn –
for he has done it.

Yet Christian eyes cannot read this psalm, nor Christian li
sing it, without applying it to the sufferings of Christ and F
subsequent glory. Not only did Jesus quote its opening wor
as one of His seven sayings from the cross (Matthew 27:4
Mark 15:34), but the mockery of verses 7 and 8 was echoed
the priests (Matthew 27:39-44; Mark 15:31-32; Luke 23:3.
the division of clothing in verse 18 was said to be fulfilled
the soldiers (John 19:23,24), and verse 22 is applied to Chr
in Hebrews 2:11,12. Further, the sufferer's agony in verses
to 17 – his disjointed bones, his thirst and his pierced han
and feet – is a remarkable description of the horrors
crucifixion, although it is not quoted of Christ in the New T
tament.

The psalm is in two contrasting parts.

The cry of anguish (verses 1-21)

The sufferer cries out to God in an agonised question: W
have you forsaken me? His greatest suffering is neither t
physical pain, nor the mockery of his persecutors, which
will later describe, but his sense of God-forsakenness. F
question is asked in perplexity, not in despair or bitterne
Indeed, the poignancy of his condition is that he continues
faith to appeal to God three times as my God even while he
forsaken and receives no reply.

Three thoughts seem to aggravate his condition and at t
same time buttress his faith. He expresses them in the ne
paragraphs. First, there was the experience of the ancier
(verses 3-5). He knows that God is holy, separate from a
exalted above all other beings, because the fathers trusted
Him and cried to Him, and they were delivered, not disa
pointed. Secondly, there are the taunts of his enemies (verses
8), who mock him because his experience is not like that of t
fathers: He trusts in the LORD; let the LORD rescue him. W
God allow them thus to blaspheme Him? Thirdly, the psalm
looks back to his own past experience of God (verses 9-1
Jehovah has been his God from his birth; He will surely n
abandon him now. These thoughts lead him to a piteo
appeal to God (verse 11) that he will not be far away, sin
trouble is close at hand.

What precisely is his trouble? He is evidently very sic
indeed dying, fast approaching the dust of death (verse 15). I
portrays the physical symptoms he both sees and feels (vers
14,15).

But his bodily pains are made worse by the band of evil m
(verse 16) who surround him. He has already likened them
strong bulls from the rich pasture-land of Bashan and to lio
ready to devour him (verses 12,13). Now he pictures them
savage pariah dogs (verse 16), and later as wild oxen (verse 2

waiting to tear him limb from limb. In some brutal way they pierce his hands and feet; they *stare and gloat* over him (verse 17); they even strip him of his clothes and share them out (verse 18), or have done so mentally in anticipation of his death. For the third time (see verses 1,2, and 11) he appeals to God to draw near to him in his need and to deliver him (verses 19-21).

The song of praise (verses 22-31)

Suddenly and dramatically the tone of the psalm changes from prayer to praise, from suffering to triumph. God's deliverance of the sufferer is not described. We are simply told (verse 24) that in the end God has *not despised* His afflicted servant, as men had despised him (verse 6), but has heard his cry when he called to Him. The psalmist's soul is so transported with adoration that he wants everybody to praise God with him. The true worshipper is always thus missionary-minded; he cannot conceive of praising God alone. In the remaining verses of the psalm the circle of those who are summoned to the worship of God grows ever wider until finally it embraces all nations and all ages.

First, he will declare and praise God's name in the great assembly (verses 22-25). He means to bear public witness to God's deliverance among his fellow Israelites, the *descendants of Jacob*, and offer Him public praise. Next, he seems to think of his fellow-sufferers, others who are still *poor* (verse 26) or "afflicted" (Revised Standard Version) as he has been (verse 24). He wants them to share his joy and with him *eat and be satisfied*, probably in the sacrifical meal which followed a thank-offering. Next (verses 27,28) his prophetic eyes look on to the conversion of the nations, and he asserts that *All the ends of the earth will... turn to the* Lord, recognising that universal *dominion belongs* to him.

Even this glorious prospect does not exhaust his vision. Although verse 29 is acknowledged as obscure and may bring together either the proud and the humble who realise their mortality, or the living and the dead, yet verses 30 and 31 contain a clear reference to the psalmist's *posterity*. They too, *a people yet unborn*, shall hear of the Lord and of His salvation. Thus, the publishing of the gospel of salvation is to be both universal and everlasting, and we see dimly foreshadowed in the results of this godly man's sufferings the final triumph of the Crucified.

Psalm 23

The Lord is My Shepherd

There are, in this best known and best loved of all psalms, two graphic pictures of God's intimate relationship with one of His people. The first is the shepherd and his sheep, the second the host and his guest.

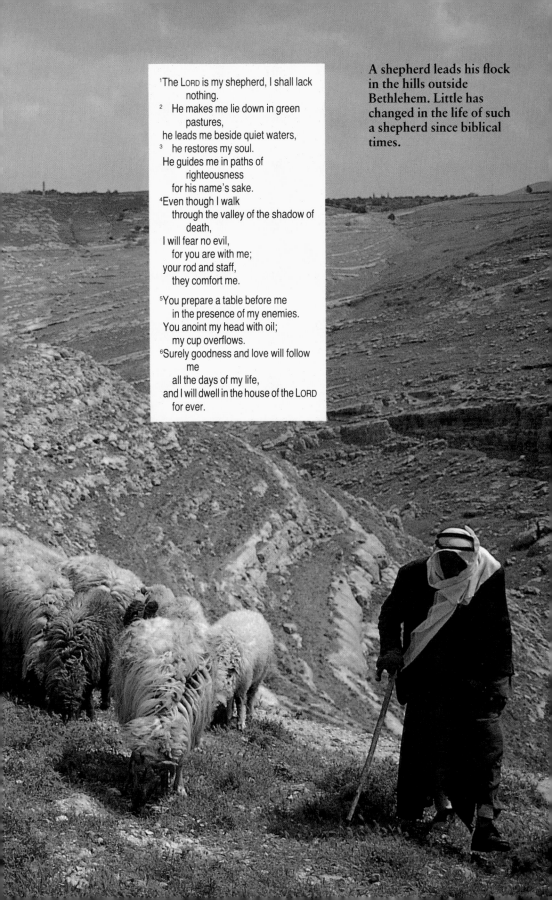

¹The LORD is my shepherd, I shall lack
    nothing.
²   He makes me lie down in green
        pastures,
he leads me beside quiet waters,
³   he restores my soul.
He guides me in paths of
        righteousness
    for his name's sake.
⁴Even though I walk
    through the valley of the shadow of
        death,
I will fear no evil,
    for you are with me;
your rod and staff,
    they comfort me.

⁵You prepare a table before me
    in the presence of my enemies.
You anoint my head with oil;
    my cup overflows.
⁶Surely goodness and love will follow
        me
    all the days of my life,
and I will dwell in the house of the LORD
    for ever.

A shepherd leads his flock
in the hills outside
Bethlehem. Little has
changed in the life of such
a shepherd since biblical
times.

The Lord my shepherd (verses 1-4)

It was natural for a pastoral community to think of the Lord their shepherd, who *brought his people out like a flock; he l[ed] them like sheep through the desert* (Psalm 78:52; see al[so] Psalm 80:1; Isaiah 40:11). But here the metaphor is ma[de] unmistakably personal. *The LORD is my shepherd*, the writ[er] boldly claims, and does not even mention the other sheep [in] the flock.

The Christian cannot read or sing this psalm without thin[k]ing of Jesus Christ, who dared to reapply the metaphor fro[m] Jehovah to Himself. It is He who is to us "the good shepherd" "the Chief Shepherd," and "that great Shepherd of the shee[p]" (John 10:11,14; 1 Peter 5:4; Hebrews 13:20).

Once I can say from personal experience *the LORD is [my] shepherd*, I can add with assurance the consequence: *I sh[all] lack nothing*. The Good Shepherd cares for His sheep and provides for all my needs. He makes me lie down in green pa[s]tures to satisfy my hunger, and leads me beside refreshing wa[t]ers to quench my thirst (verse 2). *For his name's sake*, that [is] out of loyalty to His character and promises, He will guide [me] *in the paths of righteousness;* that is, He will not allow me [to] go astray (verse 3).

Indeed, even when I walk *through the darkest valley* (alte[r]native translation, verse 4), whether that be death or so[me] other sombre place, I have nothing to fear and I will not fea[r] because my Shepherd is *with me*, protecting me with His cl[ub] and guiding me with His staff (verse 4). My security lies n[ot] then, in my environment — whether green pastures and st[ill] waters or the darkest valley — but in my Shepherd. In His pr[e]sence there is neither want (verse 1) nor fear (verse 4).

The Lord my host (verses 5,6)

The scene changes. I am no longer out of doors, but indoor[s] no longer a sheep in a flock, but a guest at a banquet. My divi[ne] host has prepared *a table before me*. It is not a secret feast, b[ut] enjoyed in the presence of my enemies, because when [He] satisfies the soul, it cannot be hidden from the world.

His provision is wonderfully lavish — a table laden wi[th] food, perfumed oils to anoint my head, and an overflowi[ng] cup (verse 5). Moreover, what God has begun He will sure[ly] continue. As He Himself will *lead me* (verses 2,3), so His *goo[d]ness and love will follow me*. Thus He will guard me behi[nd] and before, throughout *all the days of my life*. Finally, *I w[ill] dwell in the house of the LORD for ever* — not indeed in t[he] Tabernacle or the Temple, nor even just in His presence in th[is] life, but in that Father's house with its many mansions, [of] which Jesus spoke, where He said He was going to prepare [a] place for His own (John 14:1-4).

Psalm 24

Ascending the Hill of the Lord

The most probable historical setting for this psalm is the triumphant occasion described in 2 Samuel 6 when King David brought the ark from the house of Obed-edom into the tent which he had pitched for it in Jerusalem. It is probable that an annual Jewish festival commemorated either this event or God's choice of David and of Jerusalem, and that during it the ark was carried into the city and this psalm was sung.

Whatever the occasion, it is not difficult to imagine a processional choir singing it as they approached the Temple on Mount Zion, with the questions and answers of verses 3 and 4, and 7 to 10, chanted antiphonally as is sometimes done with effect by choirs today.

The whole earth (verses 1,2)

The psalm opens with a grand statement that the whole earth, with all its inhabitants, belongs to the Lord (verse 1) because He is its creator (verse 2): He has *founded it upon the seas* and *established it upon the waters*. This description of the land floating on the sea is of course poetic and is perhaps based on the account in Genesis 1 of the appearance of the dry land out of the sea. It is not misleading even today (figuratively speaking) when we consider that about seventy per cent of the earth's surface consists of water. The statement in verse 1 that the earth and its contents belong to God is quoted by Paul in 1 Corinthians 10:26 to support his argument that Christians may eat any food, even idol meats.

¹The earth is the LORD's, and
everything in it,
the world, and all who live in it;
²for he founded it upon the seas
and established it upon the waters.

³Who may ascend the hill of the LORD?
Who may stand in his holy place?
⁴He who has clean hands and a pure
heart,
who does not lift up his soul to an idol
or swear by what is false.

⁵He will receive blessing from the LORD
and vindication from God our
Saviour.
⁶Such is the generation of those who
seek him,
who seek your face, O God of Jacob.
Selah

⁷Lift up your heads, O you gates;
be lifted up, you ancient doors,
that the King of glory may come in.
⁸Who is the King of glory?
The LORD strong and mighty,
the LORD mighty in battle.

⁹Lift up your heads, O you gates;
lift them up, you ancient doors,
that the King of glory may come in.
¹⁰Who is he, this King of glory?
The LORD Almighty –
he is the King of glory.   *Selah*

The Lord's hill (verses 3-6)

Although the whole earth is the Lord's, there is a certain hill which is His in a special sense. Called *the hill of the Lord* (verse 3) and *his holy place*, it is Mount Zion where the ark, the symbol of His presence, was housed. But *who may ascend* there into His holy presence (verse 3)? The answer, which is reminiscent of Psalm 15, expresses that union of worship and morality which is constantly insisted on in the Bible.

The only worship which is acceptable to God is that offered by people who have *clean hands and a pure heart* (verse 4), that is, who are holy in thought and motive as well as in deed.

e Dome of the Rock
l the old city of
usalem from the Mount
Olives. The Dome of
Rock stands over the
e of the Jewish Temple
iblical times.

Moreover, their holiness characterises their relationship with both God and others, for they do not *lift up (their) soul to an idol*, nor have they sworn *by what is false,* deceiving their neighbor. It is such people, godly and just, who will receive God's blessing and acceptance (verse 5); indeed, such blessing is the portion of all those *who seek your face, O God of Jacob* (verse 6).

The city gates (verses 7-10)
The procession bearing the ark has now reached the gates of the city of David, and the voices of the choir ring out: *Lift up your heads, O you gates... that the King of glory may come in* (verse 7). Back comes the challenge from inside the city: *Who is this King of glory?* to which the choir responds: *The LORD strong and mighty, the LORD mighty in battle* (verse 8). The whole dialogue is then repeated word for word (verses 9,10), except that in the final response *the King of glory* is now further described as *the LORD Almighty.* It is the first time that this title occurs in the Psalter, and it forms a splendid climax to this psalm.

Opposite: Waterfall at En Gedi, on the western shore of the Dead Sea. The Hebrew name means "Goats' Spring", and En Gedi was known well to the psalmist, David.

Psalm 27

The Soul's Changing Moods

The assertions and petitions of this psalm are made against the background of many enemies. If David was its author (which there seems no adequate reason to question), the situation described is likely to be either his pursuit by Saul or his flight from Absalom. In any case, the enemies are *evil men* (verse 2) persecuting him for righteousness' sake, and seeking to harm him by physical violence and by slander (verse 14). He likens them to wild beasts eager to tear him limb from limb (verse 2).

Confidence in God (verses 1-7)

The psalm opens with one of the most sublime Old Testament affirmations of the security of God's people. *The LORD is my light*, to guide me, *my salvation*, to deliver me, and *the stronghold of my life*, in whom I take refuge. *Of whom*, then, shall

¹The LORD is my light and my salvation –
 whom shall I fear?
The LORD is the stronghold of my life –
 of whom shall I be afraid?
²When evil men advance against me
 to devour my flesh,
when my enemies and my foes attack
 me,
 they will stumble and fall.
³Though an army besiege me,
 my heart will not fear;
though war break out against me,
 even then will I be confident.

⁴One thing I ask of the LORD,
 this is what I seek:
that I may dwell in the house of the
 LORD
 all the days of my life,
to gaze upon the beauty of the LORD
 and to seek him in his temple.
⁵For in the day of trouble
 he will keep me safe in his dwelling;
he will hide me in the shelter of his
 tabernacle
 and set me high upon a rock.
⁶Then my head will be exalted
 above the enemies who surround
 me;
at his tabernacle will I sacrifice with
 shouts of joy;
 I will sing and make music to the
 LORD.

⁷Hear my voice when I call, O LORD;
 be merciful to me and answer me.
⁸My heart says of you, "Seek his face!"
 Your face, LORD, I will seek.
⁹Do not hide your face from me,
 do not turn your servant away in
 anger;
 you have been my helper.
Do not reject me or forsake me,
 O God my Saviour.
¹⁰Though my father and mother forsake
 me,
 the LORD will receive me.
¹¹Teach me your way, O LORD;
 lead me in a straight path
 because of my oppressors.
¹²Do not hand me over to the desire of
 my foes,
 for false witnesses rise up against
 me,
 breathing out violence.

¹³I am still confident of this:
 I will see the goodness of the LORD
 in the land of the living.
¹⁴Wait for the LORD;
 be strong and take heart
 and wait for the LORD.

I be afraid? It is a defiant, unanswerable question reminisce
of those at the end of Romans 8. Let David's enemies atta
him, yet *they will stumble and fall* (verse 2). Indeed (verse
if a whole army should make war against him, *even then*
will be *confident.*

Many Christians, surrounded by foes, have drawn streng
from these words. One such was James Hannington, fir
Bishop of Equatorial Africa. In October 1885, on reachir
Lake Victoria Nyanza, he was seized and imprisoned. "Co
sumed with fever, and at times delirious with pain, devour
by vermin, menaced every moment by the prospect of death,
found strength in the Psalms." On October 28, the day befo
he died a martyr's death, he wrote in his journal: "I am qui
broken down and brought low. Comforted by Psalm 27."

This steadfast assurance of one man against many foes
now further explained. It lies in the presence and the prote
tion of God. David cherishes one desire above all others (ver
4), namely to *dwell in the house of the* LORD all his life, so th
he may both *gaze upon the beauty of the* LORD or "savour t
sweetness of the Lord" and *seek him in his temple.*

It is most unlikely that we are intended to interpret th
ambition literally. Only the priests lived in the precincts
God's house, whether what is here meant is the tabernacle
Shiloh or on Mount Zion, and David could not have aspired
the priesthood since he belonged to the tribe of Judah, not t
tribe of Levi. So we must interpret the language figuratively
a noble longing to enjoy unbroken communion with God,
order to worship His glory and discern His will. Compa
Psalm 23:5,6 for a similar reference to the house of God.

It was through such a life of abiding in God that David kne
he would be delivered. *In the day of trouble* God would prote
him, as a tent gives the traveler shelter from the sun or a hig
rock safety from the floods (verses 5,6). For such deliveran
he will praise God in His Tabernacle (literally this time) wi
sacrifices and *shouts of joy* (verse 6).

Crying to God (verses 8-16)
Suddenly everything is different. The main verbs change fro
the third person to the second and from a statement to
prayer. The mood alters too, as confident affirmation giv

place to an anxious supplication to God. So abrupt and complete is the change that some commentators have ascribed the two halves of the Psalm to different authors, or, if to the same author, at least to different occasions and circumstances. Yet those who know something of the soul's moods, of the ebb and flow of faith, and of the alternating rhythm of praise and prayer, will see no necessity for this double ascription.

David prays, seeking not only God's ear, but His face (verses 7,8). He is encouraged to do so because of God's own invitation. When God says: *Seek my face* (see margin), his heart responds: *Your face, LORD, I will seek.* True prayer is never a presumptuous approach to God, but rather a response to His gracious initiative. It is this assurance which prompts David to add: *Do not hide your face from me* (verse 9). Although he seems to recognise that his sins deserve only God's displeasure, he is sure that God, who has been his help in the past, will not now cast him off (verse 10). Even were his own parents to forsake him, he says, *the Lord will receive me* (verse 10), or "adopt me as his child," as one commentator puts it. For the likeness of God's love in the Old Testament to the tender care of a father or mother see Psalm 103:13; Isaiah 49:15; 63:16.

The negative prayer not to be forsaken is now followed by a positive petition for guidance, that his steps may be directed on to a level path. He desires to be taught God's way (verse 13), lest he be delivered into the will of his adversaries (verse 14).

The psalm ends as it began with an expression of serene confidence. The author has come through his tunnel of darkness. His faith has been sorely tried, but now it triumphs; *I am still confident of this: I will see the goodness of the LORD in the land of the living* (verse 15). He who ardently desired to see with the eye of faith the beauty of the Lord (verse 4) is sure that, before he dies, he will see the same Lord's goodness displayed in his own circumstances. So certain is he of this that he urges others to *wait for the LORD* (verse 14), that is, to trust patiently in Him. It is not enough to urge people to *be strong* and *take heart* (verse 14). These would be empty sentiments unless they are both prefaced and followed by the other injunction to *wait for the LORD*. Courage can be no more than a Stoic virtue. It is only Christian when it is the fruit of a quiet confidence in God.

Psalm 29

The Voice of the Lord

A violent thunderstorm causes most people spasms of fear.
Not so the Hebrew psalmist, who sees it rather as a manifestation of the glory of God. So convinced is he that God is in control of the elements, that he resorts to a bold anthropomorph-
ism and calls the thunder *the voice of the LORD*. We must not
imagine that he wants us to take him literally, any more than
in other psalms, where the wind is His "breath," the heavens
the work of His "fingers," and the animals feed from His open
"hand" (see for example Psalms 147:18; 8:3 and 104:28).
These are dramatic figures of speech for His immanent activity
in the world.

¹Ascribe to the LORD, O mighty ones,
   ascribe to the LORD glory and
   strength.
²Ascribe to the LORD the glory due to his
   name;
   worship the LORD in the splendour of
   his holiness.
³The voice of the LORD is over the
   waters;
   the God of glory thunders,
   the LORD thunders over the mighty
   waters.

⁴The voice of the LORD is powerful;
   the voice of the LORD is majestic.
⁵The voice of the LORD breaks the
   cedars;
   the LORD breaks in pieces the
   cedars of Lebanon.
⁶He makes Lebanon skip like a calf,
   Sirion like a young wild ox.
⁷The voice of the Lord strikes
   with flashes of lightning.
⁸The voice of the LORD shakes the
   desert;
   The LORD shakes the Desert of
   Kadesh.

⁹The voice of the LORD twists the oaks
   and strips the forests bare.
   And in his temple all cry, "Glory!"
¹⁰The LORD sits enthroned over the flood;
   the LORD is enthroned as King for
   ever.
¹¹The LORD gives strength to his people;
   the LORD blesses his people with
   peace.

Mount Hermon, the
highest peak in Israel.
Snow-capped for most of
the year, the mountain
reaches over 9,000 feet
(2,800 metres).

The voice of the Lord

The poet seems to be describing the course of a thunderstorm as it comes from the north of Palestine (Lebanon and Sirion, or Mount Hermon, verses 5,6) and passes overhead to vent its fury upon the *Desert of Kadesh* in the far south (verse 8). Seven times *the voice of the LORD* is mentioned. One writer compares it to "successive peals of thunder," which reverberate over the countryside. At first it is heard *over the waters* (verse 3), which seems to mean "above the rainclouds," *powerful and majestic*

Opposite: "The voice of
the LORD is over the
waters... the voice of the
LORD is majestic."

(verse 4). But then the thunder comes closer, and the stor
brings havoc in its train, breaking down the mighty *cedars*
Lebanon, and making the mountain itself shake till it seems
skip like a calf... like a young wild ox (verse 6). The peals
thunder are accompanied by flashes of forked lightning (ver
7). The deer give premature birth to their young (see margir
and the forests are stripped bare by the hurricane (verse 9).
evident is the presence of God that the earth seems like F
temple. Awestruck by His majesty, all cry *Glory!*

The glory of the Lord
This is one of several nature psalms. But it would be a gra
mistake to suppose that the psalmist's intention is merely
give a poetic description of the beauties of nature. His wor
view is essentially God-centred. He is interested in sun a
stars (Psalms 8,19), thunder and lightning (Psalm 29), bir
and beasts (Psalm 104), only because they speak to him of t
greatness and the goodness of God. In Psalm 29 this is pla
from the introduction and the conclusion.

The introduction (verses 1,2) is a summons to the *migh*
ones to ascribe sovereignty to God. These "mighty ones" a
angels, as is plain from Psalm 89:6 and Job 1:6; 2:1; 38:
They *ascribe to the LORD the glory due to his name* (verse .
He is *the God of glory,* and His glory is partly manifest in t
solemn magnificence of a thunderstorm.

If the introduction exhorts the angels in heaven to worsh
God, the conclusion is a prayer that this same God will bl
His people on earth. His power to do so is undoubted, for I
sits enthroned *over the flood* and reigns as *king for ever* (ver
10). The transition from the description of the thundersto
to the blessing of the people is important, because it shows th
the Jews were aware of no dichotomy between nature a
grace. The God of the thunder was the God of Israel, soverei
over the elements as over the affairs of men and nations. T
sanctuary was not only in Jerusalem, for the forest and the w
derness were his temple, in which he could be worshiped.
thunderstorm was not an alien phenomenon. Had not Jehov
revealed Himself to His covenant people at Mount Sinai
thunder and lightning (Exodus 19:16; 20:18)? Yet He, who
voice is heard in the thunder, can also pacify the storm, maki
Himself known in the still small voice as well as in the eart
quake (1 Kings 19:11,12). He is thus able to give to His peop
not only *strength* but *peace* (verse 10).

Psalm 32
The Forgiveness and Guidance of God

The last two verses of this psalm form a good introduction
it. They contain the familiar, uncompromising biblical co
trast between the *wicked* and the *righteous,* the believer ar
the unbeliever. The particular difference between them me
tioned here is that, whereas *the woes of the wicked* are man
the righteous can *rejoice in the LORD and be glad.* It is furth
made clear that the ground of the joy of believers is that God
unfailing love surrounds them. Human joy arises from God
love, and the rest of the psalm unfolds its outworking in H
forgiveness and guidance of the sinner.

God's forgiveness of the past (verses 1-8)
The psalm begins with two Old Testament beatitudes, affirm
ing the blessedness not now of the person whose delight is
God's law (verses 1,2), but of the person whose sins are forg
ven. First, the facts of sin and forgiveness are described, in ea
case by three expressions. Wrong-doing is *transgression,* inc
cating a positive offence, a trespass, the stepping over a know
boundary; and *sin*, a negative missing of the mark, an omi
sion, the failure to attain an ideal; and "iniquity" (Revis
Standard Version), that inward moral perversity or corrupti
of nature which we call "original sin."
   Forgiveness is threefold too. The Hebrew word translat
forgiven in verse 1 apparently means to remove or to lift. Sin
also *covered,* put out of sight; and therefore the Lord refuses

¹Blessed is he
   whose transgressions are forgiven,
   whose sins are covered.
²Blessed is the man
   whose sin the LORD does not count
      against him
   and in whose spirit is no deceit.

³When I kept silent,
   my bones wasted away
   through my groaning all day long.
⁴For day and night
   your hand was heavy upon me;
my strength was sapped
   as in the heat of summer.   *Selah*

⁵Then I acknowledged my sin to you
   and did not cover up my iniquity.
I said, "I will confess
   my transgressions to the LORD" –
and you forgave
   the guilt of my sin.   *Selah*

⁶Therefore let everyone who is godly
   pray to you
   while you may be found;
surely when the mighty waters rise,
   they will not reach him.
⁷You are my hiding place;
   you will protect me from trouble
   and surround me with songs of
      deliverance.   *Selah*

⁸I will instruct you and teach
   you in the way you should go;
   I will counsel you and watch over
      you.
⁹Do not be like the horse or the mule,
   which have no understanding
   but must be controlled by bit and bridle
   or they will not come to you.
¹⁰Many are the woes of the wicked,
   but the LORD's unfailing love
   surrounds the man who trusts in him.

¹¹Rejoice in the LORD and be glad, you
      righteous;
   sing, all you who are upright in heart!

reckon it against the sinner. Forgiveness is thus regarded as the lifting of a burden, the covering of an ugly sight, and the cancelling of a debt. It is these verses which the apostle Paul quoted in Romans 4:6-8 as an Old Testament example of God's justification of the sinner by His grace through faith, altogether apart from works.

From this general statement of the blessedness of being forgiven, David turns to a description from personal experience of the misery of refusing to confess sin. He has written of the person *in whose spirit is no deceit* (verse 2), but now he depicts the painful consequences of deceit.

The reference is probably to his shameful dealings with Bathsheba, since, after committing adultery with her and murdering her husband, it was almost a year before he was brought to repentance by the ministry of the prophet Nathan (2 Samuel 11). During this period, while he tried to deceive himself and God, he had no peace. Indeed, long before the term "psychosomatic medicine" was coined, David tells how remorse and a tortured conscience resulted in alarming physical symptoms (verses 3,4). But at last he gave in, acknowledged his sin to God and found peace through forgiveness (verse 5).

David's vivid experience of forgiveness through repentance and confession leads him to urge others to do what he did and so receive what he received. Humble prayer to God, at a time when He may be found, always brings relief (verse 6). Moreover, David resolves constantly to do the same himself (verse 7). He has learned his lesson; he will not make the same mistake again.

The Church of the
Beatitudes, on the
northern shore of the Sea
of Galilee. The church is
built on the traditional site
of Jesus's Sermon on the
Mount.

God's guidance for the future (verses 8,9)

David's expression of confidence in God to preserve him (verse 8) is immediately answered. God gives him a promise of personal guidance, for in His steadfast love He is concerned not only to forgive the past but also to direct the future. God's guidance, like His forgivenesss, is expressed in four verbs: *I will instruct you and teach you in the way you should go; I will counsel you and watch over you* (verse 8). The picture seems to be of a mother teaching her child to walk. She never takes her eye off the child. Our God is just as tender and loving toward His people.

Nevertheless, it is important to see that verse 9 follows verse 8. God's promise of guidance is not intended to save us the bother of using our own intelligence. So to His promise he adds the command: *Do not be like the horse or the mule, which have no understanding but must be controlled by bit and bridle.* The sensitive horse and the stubborn mule have to be controlled and guided by pressure, even by force, because they are irrational animals. But we have been given a mind; we must not expect God to use a bit and bridle in His handling of us. He will treat us like human beings, not mules.

Blessed indeed are those who are surrounded by the steadfast love of God, forgiving their sins when they confess them to Him, and guiding their footsteps when they trust His promise and obey His command to use their mind.

Psalm 34

Boasting in God

One of the notable features of this psalm is its combination of worship and witness. In answer to prayer the psalmist has been marvellously delivered by God from some great peril, and his gratitude brims over now in praise, now in exhortation to others to taste and see the Lord's goodness for themselves. He describes himself as "boasting in the LORD" (verse 2). That is, he ascribes his salvation to the Lord, and because he does so out loud, those who hear him will give the glory to God too. C.H.Spurgeon, the great Baptist preacher, said: "The first ten verses are a hymn, and the last twelve a sermon."

A personal experience (verses 1-10)
The author is determined that his praise shall be not only continuous (verse 1) but congregational (verses 2,3). Since it is *in the LORD* alone (emphatic) that his soul boasts, he knows that *the afflicted* will *hear and rejoice*, for this is the only kind of boasting which makes the humble glad. So he invites them to glorify the Lord with him (verse 3), as later he urges them to look to the Lord themselves and become *radiant* (verse 5).

The reason for his worship, and his summons to others to worship, is some particular and personal experience in which he cried to God and was delivered from all his fears (verse 4)

will extol the LORD at all times;
his praise will always be on my lips.
My soul will boast in the LORD;
let the afflicted hear and rejoice.
Glorify the LORD with me;
let us exalt his name together.

sought the LORD, and he answered me;
he delivered me from all my fears.
Those who look to him are radiant;
their faces are never covered with shame.
This poor man called, and the LORD heard him; .
he saved him out of all his troubles.
The angel of the LORD encamps around those who fear him,
and he delivers them.
aste and see that the LORD is good;
blessed is the man who takes refuge in him.

⁹Fear the LORD, you his saints,
for those who fear him lack nothing.
¹⁰The lions may grow weak and hungry,
but those who seek the LORD lack no good thing.

¹¹Come, my children, listen to me;
I will teach you the fear of the LORD.
¹²Whoever of you loves life
and desires to see many good days,
¹³keep your tongue from evil
and your lips from speaking lies.
¹⁴Turn from evil and do good;
seek peace and pursue it.

¹⁵The eyes of the LORD are on the righteous
and his ears are attentive to their cry;
¹⁶the face of the LORD is against those who do evil,
to cut off the memory of them from the earth.

¹⁷The righteous cry out, and the LORD hears them;
he delivers them from all their troubles.
¹⁸The LORD is close to the brokenhearted
and saves those who are crushed in spirit.

¹⁹A righteous man may have many troubles,
but the LORD delivers him from them all;
²⁰he protects all his bones,
not one of them will be broken.

²¹Evil will slay the wicked;
the foes of the righteous will be condemned.
²²The LORD redeems his servants;
no-one who takes refuge in him will be condemned.

and all his troubles (verse 6). He is evidently himself the po[or]
man of verse 6. What the situation was out of which God de[li]
vered him the psalmist does not tell us.

Whatever the nature of the psalmist's distress, out of whi[ch]
he has been rescued, he is confident that God can do for oth[ers]
what He has done for him. *The angel of the LORD* (an Old T[es]
tament expression which often seems to indicate the prese[nce]
of God Himself) encircles those who fear Him, as an ar[my]
camps round a city to protect and deliver it (verse 7). So s[ure]
of this is the psalmist, that he appeals to others to *taste and* [see]
for themselves and to *fear the LORD*, since those who fear H[im]
lack nothing (verses 8,9). Even the *lions*, singled out as "[the]
strongest beasts of prey, most capable of providing for the[m]
selves", sometimes go hungry, but God's trusting people w[ill]
lack no good thing (verse 10).

The repeated references to "fear" in these verses [are]
noteworthy. Deliverance from their fears (verse 4) is promis[ed]
to those who fear the Lord (verses 7,9). This truth is nea[tly]
expressed in Tate and Brady's popular hymn paraphrasing t[his]
psalm, "Through All the Changing Scenes of Life:"

> *Fear him, you saints, and you will then*
> *have nothing else to fear;*
> *his service shall be your delight,*
> *your needs shall be his care.*

To fear God is not, of course, to be frightened of Him. [The]
meaning here is plain from its equivalents, namely, to "see[k]"
Him (verse 4), to "call" to Him (verse 6) and "take refug[e]"
in Him (verse 8), acknowledging our helplessness and looki[ng]
to Him for deliverance (compare Luke 1:50).

A general instruction (verses 11-22)

The psalmist's particular deliverance through the fear of [the]
Lord leads him to a general instruction based upon his exp[eri]
ence. Like the Preacher in the early chapters of the Book [of]
Proverbs, he summons his pupils to gather round him, [and]
chooses an appropriate theme (verse 11). If they desire m[any]
good days (verse 12), their fear of God must express itself [not]
just in faith, but in works, that is, in moral behavior. No [one]
can claim to fear God who does not depart from evil (comp[are]
Job 1:1; Proverbs 16:6) both in word (verse 13) and in d[eed]
(verse 14). Nor is it enough to turn away from evil; we m[ust]
positively *do good* and patiently pursue peace (verse 14).

Verses 15 to 18 describe the blessings which are grante[d]
the righteous, that is, to those who fear God, shun evil, and [do]
good. God's eyes and ears are directed toward them, while [His]
face is turned away from the wicked (verses 15,16). He he[ars]
and delivers the righteous, draws near to the *brokenheart[ed]*
and saves the *crushed in spirit* (verses 17,18).

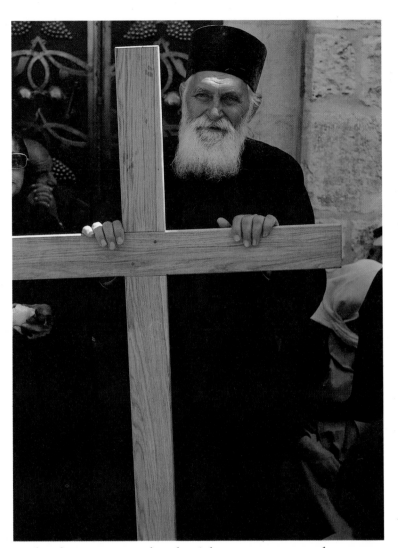

On Good Friday
Christians of every
denomination follow the
traditional route that Jesus
took through the streets of
Jerusalem on the way to
the cross.

This does not mean that the righteous are exempt from trouble. On the contrary, *a righteous man may have many troubles* (verse 19). Nevertheless, God limits the afflictions of his people both in their duration and in their extent. He delivers them out of their trials (verse 19) and, although they are often sorely wounded, He does not allow their bones to be broken (verse 20), which seems to be a figure of speech for utter destruction (see also Micah 3:3). In Paul's language, "We are hard pressed on every side, but not crushed" (2 Corinthians 4:8).

To the unbeliever who asserts that this claim is contradicted in experience, we can only reply that, stated as a principle of God's surveillance over His people, it is true. Moreover, the differentiation between the fate of the wicked and the destiny of the righteous will finally be manifest by divine judgment in eternity. The wicked *will be condemned*; but *no-one who takes refuge in Him will be condemned* (verses 21,22).

Psalm 40

Out of the Horrible Pit

Every Christian believer is fortified in present trial by the memory of past blessings. Because we have experienced God faithfulness in former days we are encouraged to trust Hi still. Such is the theme of this psalm, which begins with graphic description of deliverance and ends with an urge plea for continued mercy.

An account of past deliverance (verses 1-10)

The psalmist was down a *slimy pit*, full of *mud and mire*. The is no need to suppose that this was literally his plight, li Jeremiah, whose enemies let him down by ropes into a ciste until he sank into the slime (Jeremiah 38:1-13). The pit and t bog no doubt symbolise some desolate experience of sin depression or disease. In his helplessness, unable himself climb out, he *waited patiently for the LORD*, and the followi verses emphasise, stage by stage, the mighty deliverance God who first heard his cry, then stooped down and drew hi out of the mud, then set his feet securely upon rock, and fina

¹I waited patiently for the LORD;
    he turned to me and heard my cry.

²He lifted me out of the slimy pit,
    out of the mud and mire;
he set my feet on a rock
    and gave me a firm place to stand.
³He put a new song in my mouth,
    a hymn of praise to our God.
Many will see and fear
    and put their trust in the LORD.

⁴Blessed is the man
    who makes the LORD his trust,
who does not look to the proud,
    to those who turn aside to false gods.
⁵Many, O LORD my God,
    are the wonders you have done.
The things you planned for us
    no-one can recount to you;
were I to speak and tell of them
    they would be too many to declare.

⁶Sacrifice and offering you did not
    desire,
    but my ears you have pierced;
burnt offerings and sin offerings
    you did not require.

⁷Then I said, "Here I am, I have come –
    it is written about me in the scroll.
⁸To do your will, O my God, is my desire;
    your law is within my heart."

⁹I proclaim righteousness in the great
    assembly;
I do not seal my lips,
    as you know, O LORD.
¹⁰I do not hide your righteousness in my
    heart;
I speak of your faithfulness and
    salvation.
I do not conceal your love and your
    truth
from the great assembly.

¹¹Do not withhold your mercy from me, O
    LORD;
may your love and your truth always
    protect me.

¹²For troubles without number surround
    me;
my sins have overtaken me, and I
    cannot see.
They are more than the hairs of my
    head,
    and my heart fails within me.

¹³Be pleased, O LORD, to save me;
    O LORD, come quickly to help me.
¹⁴May all who seek to take my life
    be put to shame and confusion;
may all who desire my ruin
    be turned back in disgrace.
¹⁵May those who say to me, "Aha! Aha!"
    be appalled at their own shame.
¹⁶But may all who seek you
    rejoice and be glad in you;
may those who love your salvation
    always say,
    "The LORD be exalted!"

¹⁷Yet I am poor and needy;
    may the LORD think of me.
You are my help and my deliverer;
    O my God, do not delay.

put a fresh song of praise in his mouth, leading many to believe (verses 1-3).

Such an experience of salvation has several fruitful consequences, notably worship (verses 4-6), obedience (verses 7-9), and witness (verses 10-12). His worship is expressed both in exclaiming how blessed the believer is (verse 4) and how numberless are the deeds and thoughts of God (verse 5).

But true worship goes beyond verbal exclamations. It is more even than the offering of sacrifices. It involves the offering of ourselves in a life of moral obedience. (For the precedence of obedience over sacrifice see 1 Samuel 15:22; Isaiah 1:10-17; Jeremiah 7:21-26; Hosea 6:6; Micah 6:6-8). This obedience is demanded *in the scroll*, that is, the written law. It begins in our *ears*, which God has *pierced*, or literally (verse 6) "dug," so that He has enabled us to hear and grasp His will.

51

But God in grace does more even than this. If He has writt
His law in a book, that we may know it, and whispered it in
our ears, that we may understand it, He also inscribes it in o
hearts, so that we "delight to do it" (verse 8, *Revised Standa
Version*). This statement of knowing, loving and doing Goc
will, which is partially true of all His children, found its perfe
fulfilment in His incarnate Son, to whom it is applied in He
rews 10:5-9.

Salvation provokes within us, however, more than a Go
ward response of spiritual worship and moral obedience;
teaches us also to care for our fellows, that they too may he
of God's grace. So the psalmist asserts repeatedly that he h
not concealed God's *love and... truth* (that is, faithfulnes
from the great assembly but has publicly declared it (verses
10). When God sets our feet on the rock and puts His law
our ears and in our hearts, we cannot keep our lips from ma
ing His goodness known.

A prayer for present help (verses 11-17)
As in Psalm 27, the mood changes abruptly in the middle fro
affirmation to supplication, from a rehearsal of God's *lo
and... truth* to a plea that they will always preserve him. F
again the psalmist finds himself in peril and distress. *Troubl
without number* have encompassed him, and this time he do
not leave us in ignorance of their nature: *my sins have ove
taken me and I cannot see.* Indeed, they are not only too stror
for him to conquer, but too many for him to count. His hea
fails him (verse 12), and in self-despair he cries to God
deliver him (verse 13).

The psalm ends with a contrast between two different kin
of "seeker," those who *seek to take my life* and those *who se
you*, in a word, the godly and the ungodly. The ungodly betr:
their ungodliness in their persecution of the godly, and thr
times the psalmist prays for their overthrow (verses 14,1$
But for those who instead seek God and love His salvation I
desires a different destiny, namely that they may have cau
from their experience to say continually "*The* LORD I
exalted!" (verse 16). Among such he numbers himself. Left
himself, he knows he is *poor and needy*, but the Lord, who h.
been his deliverer, cares for him still and will yet deliver hi
again (verse 17).

Psalms 42, 43
The Causes and Cure of Spiritual Depression

The subject of this psalm (for Psalms 42 and 43 seem clearly to belong together) is spiritual depression, its causes and cure. The author's soul is *downcast* (verse 5), and *disturbed* within him. This is an experience by no means rare, even among godly people. Christian biographies supply many examples. Moreover, it is almost certain that our Lord Himself was alluding to these verses when He cried both "Now my heart is troubled" and "My soul is overwhelmed with sorrow" (John 12:27; Mark 14:34).

What is particularly moving is that the psalmist does not acquiesce in his condition, but three times, in words which form a refrain, he questions himself about his despondency and summons himself to trust in God (42:6,7,14,15 and 43:5, 6).

So the psalm forms three stanzas. Each begins with the psalmist's grief, in which he addresses God or his readers, and ends with the refrain, in which he addresses himself.

salm 42

s the deer pants for streams of water,
  so my soul pants for you, O God.
ly soul thirsts for God, for the living
    God.
  When can I go and meet with God?
ly tears have been my
  food day and night,
·hile men say to me all day long,
  "Where is your God?"
hese things I remember
  as I pour out my soul:
ow I used to go with the multitude,
  leading the procession to the house
    of God,
ith shouts of joy and thanksgiving
  among the festive throng.

Vhy are you downcast, O my soul?
  Why so disturbed within me?
ut your hope in God,
  for I will yet praise him,
  my Saviour and 6my God.

ly soul is downcast within me;
  therefore I will remember you
om the land of the Jordan,
  the heights of Hermon – from Mount
    Mizar.

7Deep calls to deep
  in the roar of your waterfalls;
all your waves and breakers
  have swept over me.

8By day the LORD directs his love,
  at night his song is with me –
  a prayer to the God of my life.

9I say to God my Rock,
  "Why have you forgotten me?
Why must I go about mourning,
  oppressed by the enemy?"
10My bones suffer mortal agony
  as my foes taunt me,
saying to me all day long,
  "Where is your God?"

11Why are you downcast, O my soul?
  Why so disturbed within me?
Put your hope in God,
  for I will yet praise him,
  my Saviour and my God.

Psalm 43

1Vindicate me, O God,
  and plead my cause against an
    ungodly nation;
  rescue me from deceitful and wicked
    men.
2You are God my stronghold.
  Why have you rejected me?
Why must I go about mourning,
  oppressed by the enemy?
3Send forth your light and your truth,
  let them guide me;
let them bring me to your holy
    mountain,
  to the place where you dwell.
4Then will I go to the altar of God,
  to God, my joy and my delight.
I will praise you with the harp,
  O God, my God.

5Why are you downcast, O my soul?
  Why so disturbed within me?
Put your hope in God,
  for I will yet praise him,
  my Saviour and my God.

The causes of spiritual depression

At first the author portrays himself not as cast down, but as thirsty. He thirsts for God, as a *deer* thirsts for water when overtaken by hunters or by drought. In C.S.Lewis's phrase, he has a keen "appetite for God." This is natural and right. It is, or should be, the experience of every believer. Though indeed God "satisfies the thirsty and fills the hungry with good things" (Psalm 107:9; compare Psalm 36:8,9), yet our hunger and thirst for Him are satisfied only to break out again more fiercely (compare Psalm 63:1,2).

In this case, however, the author's thirst is aggravated by two factors, which he immediately mentions. The first is

e barren wilderness of
Judean Hills; the Dead
can be seen in the
tance.

expressed in the form of a question: *When can I go and meet
with God?* (verse 2). This is what the Israelite was required to
do three times a year, visiting Jerusalem for the major festivals
(see Exodus 23:17), and this evidently the psalmist was unable
to do. Secondly, his daily diet was one of tears because men
were constantly taunting him: *Where is your God?* (verse 3).
These, then, were the causes of his depression of soul: the
absence of God to comfort him and the presence of men who
mocked him. Each stanza reverts to this double theme.

His sense of estrangement from God is due to his enforced
separation from the Temple and its worship. He writes from
northern Palestine. *Mount Mizar* (verse 6) has not been iden-
tified, but is evidently a hill in the Hermon range. From this distant hill he thinks of God's *holy mountain* (43:3) and longs to
be there again. Wistfully he remembers the sheer joy of worship in former days (verse 4).

As Psalm 42 is entitled *"A Maskil* (meaning perhaps 'a instruction') *of the Sons of Korah,"* it has been suggested th; the author may have been one of the Korahites, men descende from Korah (Levi's great-grandson), who were gatekeeper watchers, and musicians in the Temple (1 Chronicles 6:22-4! 9:17-32; 2 Chronicles 20:19). Certainly he writes here praising the Lord with his voice and his harp (42:11; 43:4 But he cannot do so now because he is in exile. Instead of th Temple music he is deafened by the thunder of waterfalls ar of mountain torrents in spate, as *deep calls to deep,* echoir across the valley. They seem to symbolise his calamities; l calls them God's *waves and breakers,* which have *swept ov* him (verse 7). He longs to take part again in the Temple wo ship by day and by night (verse 9).

So, in the third stanza, he prays that God will send out H light and His truth, which like guides in the desert will lead hi; safely back to God's hill, dwelling, and altar, so that the; again he may encounter and worship the God of his joy ar gladness (43:3,4). These sentiments need not be pressed int meaning that he supposed the Temple to be the only meetir place of the soul with God — for much of the psalm is itse addressed to God while he is in exile; what he ardently desir is a renewal of that special communion with God which he ha experienced in public worship on the great festivals.

The second cause of his depression is the scoffing of th heathen who kept asking incredulously: *Where is your Goc* (verses 3,10). It is partly that they were idolaters, serving goc they could see and touch, while *the living God* was invisib (verse 2, compare Psalm 115:2); and partly that God appeare as inactive as He was invisible, and did not immediately vind cate His people when they were oppressed by their enemi (compare Psalm 79:10). The psalmist feels forgotten (verse 9 His spirit is so sensitive that the sharp pain of the scoffer taunts seems like a mortal wound in his body (verse 10). H prays for vindication and deliverance (43:1).

It is, then, this combination of circumstances which h; brought the psalmist to depression, and even to despai people ridicule him for his faith in the living God, while the li ing God whom they mock seems indifferent and far away.

The cure for spiritual depression
Each stanza, in which the author describes his sorrowf plight, concludes with the same splendid refrain (42:5,1 43:5). It is remarkable to note how the author speaks to hin self. He will not give in to his moods. He takes himself in har and reproaches himself for his depression. He recognises th; his soul is weighed down as by a crushing burden, ar inwardly *disturbed* like the raging of the sea (Psalm 46:3). B

the deer pants for ams of water, so my pants for you, O d."

why? he asks himself. Within his repeated self-questioning is an implied rebuke. Instead of answering his own questions, or excusing himself, he immediately prescribes his remedy: he must trust or "hope" in God. He must give up his introspection and self-pity, his wistful reminiscences and his pained resentment at the mockery of his enemies.

The cure for depression is neither to look in at our grief, nor back to our past, nor round at our problems, but away and up to the living God. He is our help and our God, and if we trust Him now, we shall soon have cause to praise Him again. Thus, as one writer sums up, "faith rebukes despondency and hope triumphs over despair".

Why restless, why cast down, my soul?
Hope still, and you shall sing
The praise of him who is your God,
Your health's eternal spring.
(Tate and Brady, 1696)

Psalm 46

Immanuel, God With Us

The name of Martin Luther will always be associated with th psalm. His famous hymn *"Ein' feste Burg ist unser Gott"* is free paraphrase of it. He and Philip Melanchthon would sir it together in times of dark discouragement, and Thomas Ca lyle has made it familiar to English readers by his translatic "A Safe Stronghold our God is still." It is a sublime expressic of quiet confidence in God's sovereignty amid the upheavals nature and history.

The original context was evidently some notable deliveran of Jerusalem from the attack of heathen invaders. *The city God* (verse 4) was favored with several such deliverances. B the situation envisaged in the psalm, together with i resemblance in metaphor and phrase to some of Isaiah prophecies, suggest the overthrow of Sennacherib's army 701 B.C..

Although Hezekiah was King of Judah, he was a vassal Sennacherib and was obliged to pay tribute to him. When I rebelled, the mighty army of the Assyrians came sweeping we and south like the irresistible waves of the sea. Jerusalem w soon surrounded. Sennacherib boasted that he had shut t Hezekiah "like a caged bird" and demanded his surrender.

The situation was critical. Twenty years previously Se nacherib's predecessor had taken by storm the northern ca tal of Samaria and depopulated the land of Israel. It looked if Judah was to suffer the same fate. Hezekiah appealed to t prophet Isaiah, who spoke to him the word of the Lord: "L not be afraid... for I will defend this city to save it." Sudden and dramatically, as the secular historian Herodotus bore w ness, God intervened. "That night the angel of the Lord we

---

¹God is our refuge and strength,
  an ever present help in trouble.
²Therefore we will not fear, though the
    earth give way
  and the mountains fall into the heart
    of the sea,
³though its waters roar and foam
  and the mountains quake with their
    surging.   *Selah*

⁴There is a river whose streams make
    glad the city of God,
  the holy place where the Most High
    dwells.

⁵God is within her, she will not fall;
  God will help her at break of day.
⁶Nations are in uproar, kingdoms fall;
  he lifts his voice, the earth melts.

⁷The LORD Almighty is with us;
  the God of Jacob is our fortress.
                    Selah

⁸Come and see the works of the LORD,
  the desolations he has brought on
    the earth.

⁹He makes wars cease to the ends of
    the earth;
  he breaks the bow and shatters the
    spear,
  he burns the shields with fire.
¹⁰"Be still, and know that I am God;
  I will be exalted among the nations,
  I will be exalted in the earth."

¹¹The LORD Almighty is with us;
  the God of Jacob is our fortress.
                    Selah

out and put to death a hundred and eighty-five thousand me[n]
in the Assyrian camp. When the people got up early the ne[xt]
morning – there were all the dead bodies!" So Sennacher[ib]
withdrew. See 2 Kings 18 and 19.

The psalm is in three parts, expressing first a general co[n]-
fidence in the power and providence of God, then a particul[ar]
experience of it in the deliverance of the city, and lastly a[n]
assurance that He will establish His universal kingdom [of]
peace. The second and third stanzas are followed by the re[f]-
rain: *The LORD Almighty is with us; the God of Jacob is o[ur]
fortress* (verses 7,11). The demands of symmetry suggest th[at]
the same refrain originally concluded the first stanza also. It [is]
not only a statement of God's protection, but that He who [is]
our fortress is both the powerful *LORD Almighty* and the fait[h]-
ful *God of Jacob*, who is bound to His people in a solem[n]
covenant.

A general confidence (verses 1-3)

The psalmist affirms that *God is our refuge and strength* a[nd]
an ever present help in trouble. It is this confidence which en[a]-
bles him to add almost with defiance: *Therefore we will n[ot]
fear.* Even the worst convulsions of nature – earthquak[e,]
storm, and tempest – which strike terror into the hearts [of]
defenseless people, will not make us afraid (verses 2,3).

A special experience (verses 4-7)

In contrast to the sea whose waters *roar and foam* (verse 3), t[he]
psalmist now mentions other and calmer waters, those [of]
a river whose streams make glad the city of God (verse 4[).]
The original reference must be to the waters of Siloam, who[se]
gentle flowing Isaiah used as a picture of the quiet, benefice[nt]
providence of God (Isaiah 8:6). The symbol reappears in t[he]
visions of both Ezekiel (Ezekiel 47:1-12) and John (Revelati[on]
22:1-5).

Under God's gracious rule His city is made glad (verse 4) a[nd]
simply cannot *fall* because *God is within her* to protect a[nd]
help her (verse 5). Let the nations "roar" like the sea and kin[g]-
doms "quake" like mountains (the same verbs are used in ver[se]
6 as in verses 2 and 3), yet God has only to speak and *the ear[th]
melts* before Him. That is, before the voice of the Lord, t[he]
Assyrian army was scattered.

A final assurance (verses 8-11)

The writer now summons the people to take note of God['s]
decisive intervention in the protection of Jerusalem and t[he]
desolation of her foes (verse 8). This divine deliverance is se[en]
as a pledge and foretaste of the day when God will finally ove[r]-
throw all warmongers and establish His kingdom of peace: [He]

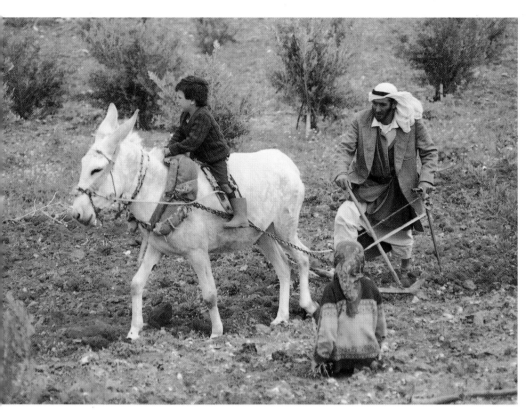

bs plow their
llholding in the
litional manner in
ky fields near the town
Bethlehem.

*breaks the bow and shatters the spear, he burns the shields
with fire* (verse 9). The vision recalls the prophecies of Isaiah
about the beating of swords into ploughshares and spears into
pruninghooks, and the using of military boots and
bloodstained garments as fuel for the fire (Isaiah 2:4; 9:5).

No sooner has this promise of peace been given than God
Himself, its guarantor, is heard to speak: *Be still, and know
that I am God.* It was His voice which overthrew the Assyrians
(verse 6); it is His voice which pacifies His people. He is God
for ever and is already here and now (probably a present tense)
exalted in the earth (verse 10). This majestic affirmation
prompts His people to respond in the refrain: *The LORD
Almighty is with us.* Again, the words have an Isaianic ring,
reminding us of his great prophecy about Immanuel, "God
with us" (Isaiah 7:14; 8:8,10).

We also live in an epoch of crisis. The old order has gone.
The social revolution begun 150 years ago continues and
grows in pace. We hear wars and rumors of wars. People's
hearts fail them for fear. Can we say: "We will not fear"?
Indeed we can; but only if we believe the other affirmations of
this psalm: *I am God* and *The LORD Almighty is with us.* As
John Wesley said with his dying breath: "The best of all is, God
is with us."

Psalm 51

Divine Mercy for the Penitent

Psalm 46 sets forth the sovereignty of God; this psalm exto
His mercy. Though He is exalted among the nations (Psal
46:10), He does not despise the broken and contrite heart of
the penitent (51:17).

    This fourth of the seven so-called "penitential psalm:
refers in its title to David's grievous sin. From his palace ro
one spring afternoon, he saw a beautiful woman name
Bathsheba, desired her for himself, and committed adulte
with her. He had her husband, Uriah the Hittite, sent into tl
hottest part of the battle with the Ammonites, where he wou
certainly be killed and, in fact, was killed. David then pro
ceeded to take her as his wife. Only when the prophet Nath;
was sent by God to rebuke him, did he feel his guilt, confess h
sin, and plead for mercy. His simple "I have sinned against tl
LORD" in 2 Samuel 12:13 is here elaborated into such a pray
for God's mercy in cleansing and renewal as has been the la
guage of penitents ever since.

The need of God's mercy

We can appreciate our need of divine mercy only when v
have seen the gravity of our sin. As in Psalm 32, so in verses
and 2 of this psalm, three separate Hebrew words are used
describe David's offence, namely *transgression* (the crossing

¹Have mercy on me, O God,
  according to your unfailing love;
  according to your great compassion
  blot out my transgressions.
²Wash away all my iniquity
  and cleanse me from my sin.

³For I know my transgressions,
  and my sin is always before me.
⁴Against you, you only, have I sinned
  and done what is evil in your sight,
  so that you are proved right when you
    speak
  and justified when you judge.
⁵Surely I have been a sinner from birth,
  sinful from the time my mother
    conceived me.
⁶Surely you desire truth in the inner
    parts;
  you teach me wisdom in the inmost
    place.

⁷Cleanse me with hyssop, and I shall be
    clean;
  wash me, and I shall be whiter than
    snow.
⁸Let me hear joy and gladness;
  let the bones you have crushed
    rejoice.
⁹Hide your face from my sins
  and blot out all my iniquity.

¹⁰Create in me a pure heart, O God,
  and renew a steadfast spirit within
    me.
¹¹Do not cast me from your presence
  or take your Holy Spirit from me.
¹²Restore to me the joy of your salvation
  and grant me a willing spirit, to
    sustain me.

¹³Then I will teach transgressors your
    ways,
  and sinners will turn back to you.

¹⁴Save me from bloodguiltiness, O God
  the God who saves me,
  and my tongue will sing of your
    righteousness.
¹⁵O Lord, open my lips,
  and my mouth will declare your
    praise.
¹⁶You do not delight in sacrifice, or I
    would bring it;
  you do not take pleasure in burnt
    offerings.
¹⁷The sacrifices of God are a broken
    spirit;
  a broken and contrite heart,
  O God, you will not despise.

¹⁸In your good pleasure make Zion
    prosper;
  build up the walls of Jerusalem.
¹⁹Then there will be righteous sacrifices
  whole burnt offerings to delight you
  then bulls will be offered on your
    altar.

a boundary), *sin* (the missing of a mark), and *iniquity* (depravity of nature). The thought behind these words is unfolded in an important recognition of the essence and origin of sin.

The essence of sin is revolt against God: *Against you, you only, have I sinned and done what is evil in your sight, so that you are proved right when you speak and justified when you judge* (verse 4). It is true that David had sinned against Bathsheba and Uriah, against his family and nation, but first and foremost, he had offended against the love and law of God. He had coveted, stolen, committed adultery and murder and, in so doing, had broken four of the five last commandments and brought himself under the just sentence of God. Compare Romans 3:4 where Paul quotes these words to establish the unswerving justice of God in His dealings with human beings. It is because we are under the judgment of God that we need the mercy of God.

If the essence of sin is rebellion, its origin is in our fallen nature: *Surely I was sinful at birth, sinful from the time my mother conceived me* (verse 5). This does not, of course, mean that the marvellous processes of conception and birth are in themselves sinful, but that our human nature from its first beginnings has been infected with sin. As we inherit it from our parents, it is twisted with self-centredness. This is "original sin," and David came to recognise it when his sinful passions of lust, jealousy, cruelty, and avarice overcame and overthrew him.

It is when we see ourselves as we are, on the one hand rebels against God and under the judgment of God, and on the other prisoners of a corrupt nature, that we come, like David, to despair of ourselves and to cry to God for mercy.

The expression of God's mercy

The mercy of God expresses itself in meeting the sinner's need, giving him both pardon and purity.

In praying for pardon, David uses two vivid metaphors. First, he asks God to *blot out* his transgressions (verses 1,9). The verb denotes the removal of writing from a book (see for example Exodus 32:32). He seems to think of his sins as a list of offences of which he is accused or a catalogue of debts which he cannot pay. He pleads that the entry be erased.

Secondly, he acknowledges that his sins have defiled him and prays that God will *wash* and *cleanse* him (verse 2), until his black stains are removed and he becomes *whiter than snow* (verse 7). Since in certain Old Testament rituals a bunch of hyssop was dipped in blood or water, which was then ceremonially sprinkled, the word *hyssop* is used in verse 7 as a symbol of cleansing.

But David knew his need of purity as well as pardon. God

demanded *truth in the inner parts* (verse 6); yet David's very nature was corrupt (verse 5). Only the creative power of God could make him a new person. So he prayed: *Create in me a pure heart, O God, and renew a steadfast spirit within me* (verse 10). He longed, that is, for a new nature with new and pure desires, and for a spirit both *steadfast* (verse 10) and *willing* (verse 12). He seems to have known too, before the full New Testament revelation had been given, that such a new nature and spirit could be imparted to him only by the Holy Spirit Himself (verse 12).

If God in mercy would grant him both a clean conscience and a clean heart, the sorrow which his sin had caused would be turned into *joy and gladness* (verse 8, compare verse 12).

The results of God's mercy

The last part of the psalm (verses 13-19) is devoted to the results which follow an experience of the cleansing and recreating mercy of God. David resolves that his attitude both to other people and to God will be different.

First, he accepts his responsibility to his fellow humans. He has sinned against them; now he will serve them in a new way. When his own transgressions have been forgiven, he will *teach transgressors* God's way, so that they return to Him (verse 13). He prays to be delivered from *bloodguilt* (verse 14). Perhaps he means that, although he has indeed been guilty of the blood of Uriah, he is determined that God shall not require at his hand the blood of sinners whom he has failed to warn and teach (compare Ezekiel 3:16-27 and 33:1-20).

His second responsibility is toward God. He will use his lips in worship as well as witness: *O Lord, open my lips, and my mouth will declare your praise* (verse 15). It is this that God desires, not *sacrifice* or *burnt offerings*. He does not mean that no sacrifice at all is pleasing to God, but that the kind of sacrifice He chiefly desires, especially from a transgressor like David, is *a broken and contrite heart*. And then, when he is forgiven, he may offer the further sacrifice of praise and thanksgiving (verse 15; compare Psalm 50:14,23).

The last two verses have seemed to many commentators not to belong to David's psalm at all. There is an apparent reference to the rebuilding of Jerusalem's walls in verse 18, although the words could be figurative. And verse 19 (*burnt offerings to delight you*) seems to contradict verse 16 (*you do not take pleasure in burnt offerings*). The discrepancy is only superficial, however, and is consistent with much teaching of both psalms and prophets. This is not that sacrifices are not acceptable to God in themselves, but that they please Him only if they are expressive of a contrite, worshiping heart and an obedient will.

Psalm 67

Saving Health to the Nations

This psalm appears to be greatly concerned about the blessing
of God. Three times in its brief seven verses it reverts to this
theme, now in prayer that God may bless us, and now in affirmation that He will do so.

This gives the psalm a rather homely touch, because we ourselves frequently talk about the blessing of God. "God bless
you," we say as we bid someone good-bye, or as we end a letter. We even utter the same prayer when people sneeze! We
seem so anxious to secure the divine blessing for our friends
that we lose no opportunity of expressing our desire for it.

Now what do we mean when we seek God's blessing? The
language of this psalm is rather beautiful because it is bor-
rowed from the words of the high priest's blessing. First given
by God to Moses, for use by Aaron and his sons in the Tabernacle worship, it is recorded in Numbers 6:24-26, "The LORD
bless you and keep you; the LORD make his face to shine upon
you and be gracious to you; the LORD turn his face towards you
and give you peace." This blessing came to be used regularly in
the Temple services at Jerusalem, and is still a favorite in Christian worship today. Echoes of it are heard in several psalms
(for instance Psalm 4:6; 29:11; 31:16; 80:3,7,55). So here
some words from the ancient blessing of Aaron form the
groundwork of this psalm, which was no doubt composed for
liturgical use in the Temple.

When read as a whole, Psalm 67 teaches us that there is some
justification for praying for ourselves, that there are unselfish
reasons for praying the selfish prayer *God bless us.* Two such
motives are given – immediate and ultimate.

¹May God be gracious to us and bless
us
and make his face to shine upon us;
Selah
²may your ways be known on earth,
your salvation among all nations.

³May the peoples praise you, O God;
may all the peoples praise you.
⁴May the nations be glad and sing for
joy,
for you rule the peoples justly
and guide the nations of the earth.
Selah

⁵May the peoples praise you, O God;
may all the peoples praise you.

⁶Then the land will yield its harvest,
and God, our God, will bless us.
⁷God will bless us,
and all the ends of the earth will fear
him.

The knowledge of God

The first reason why we desire that God shall bless us is order that through us His salvation may be known to a humankind (verses 1,2). In that case Israel's motive in seeking God's blessing was not selfish after all. They prayed that God would bless them, not in order to wallow comfortably in H blessing themselves, but in order that it might pass from the to others. They longed that God would be merciful to ther that thereby the nations might receive His mercy, and come know His ways and saving health.

We need to remember that Israel made very audacious claims for herself and her God. She claimed to be the speci people of God, with whom He had entered into an everlasting covenant. She poked fun at the dead, dumb idols of t nations. She affirmed that her God was the only living, acti and true God. So of course her heathen neighbors were watc ing her, now quizzically, now incredulously. They wanter some evidence to support Israel's contention. "Where is no your God?" they asked. They wanted to know what God cou do for His people; what difference He made to them; wheth the claims of Israel had any substance to them.

That is why Israel prayed *God be gracious to us and bless u* If only Aaron's blessing would come true! If only God's mer were granted to them! If only God were specially to bless ther and the light of His smile were to be upon them and with the always! Surely then the nations would see for themselve Then the nations would have visual proof of the existenc activity and grace of God? Then the nations would come know His way and His salvation, and experience themselv that God rules righteously and leads His people like a shephei (verse 4).

The same principle operates today. Non-Christian peop are watching us. We claim to know, to love and to follow Jes Christ. We say that he is our Savior, our Lord, and our Frien "What difference does he make to these Christians?" t world asks searchingly. "Where is their God?" It may be sa without fear of contradiction that the greatest hindrance evangelism in the world today is the failure of the church supply evidence in her own life and work of the saving pow of God. Rightly may we pray for ourselves that we may ha God's blessing and mercy and the light of His countenance not that we may then monopolize His grace and bask in t sunshine of His favor, but that others may see in us His ble sing and His beauty, and be drawn to Him through us.

The worship of God

Verses 3-5 form another refrain in this psalm. They give t second reason why we desire God's blessing. It is not just order that others may come to know Him. For why do we want them to know God? Just for their own benefit? Just that they may receive His salvation? Are we wanting others to do what we have renounced ourselves? We are not asking God's blessing for our selfish ends; are we content that others should receive His blessing for theirs? That hardly makes sense.

We need to look beyond the salvation of the nations to its ultimate purpose, which is that they too should come to worship and praise God. We should desire their salvation not just that they shall know Him for themselves, but that they shall praise Him for Himself. The greatest incentive in all evangelism is not the need of human beings but the glory of God; not that they shall receive salvation, but that they shall give to God the honor that is due to His name, acknowledging and adoring Him for ever. We cannot be content until every convert has become a worshiper.

...onk sweeps the ...dens of the lakeside ...lilee church which ...mmemorates the ...pearance of the risen ...rist to the apostles. It ...s on that occasion that ...instructed Peter: "Feed ...lambs."

Psalm 73
The Prosperity of the Wicked

The providence of God, His moral ordering of the world, is problem which has always baffled the human mind. The boo of Job and Psalms 37 and 49 as well as 73 are devoted to th theme. The problem can be simply stated. God has reveal Himself as good and just, punishing wickedness and rewar ing goodness. If He is all-powerful as well as all-good, wh does He allow such a morally perverse state of affairs to co tinue on earth? Far from justice catching up on the wicke they flourish "like a green tree" (Psalm 37:35). They not on get away with their wickedness but seem to be exempt from t troubles which befall other people. In a word, honesty is n the best policy. It does not pay to be good. It is the wicked wh prosper, while adversity overtakes the righteous. Such is t background to this psalm.

The problem (verses 1-14)
The psalmist begins with the conviction held by all godl people, even in the face of apparently contradictory circun stances: *Surely God is good... to those who are pure in hea* (verse 1). This is an axiom of revealed religion and cannot o any account be surrendered. *But as for me,* he immediatel continues, *my feet had almost slipped; I had nearly lost m foothold. For I envied* the arrogant when I saw the prosperi of the wicked (verses 2,3). First, he was troubled by the immunity to disease and disaster (verses 4,5). Next, by the arrogance (verses 6-9). Their eyes and heart, their talk an looks (verses 7,8) are full of conceit. Not only do *their tongu take possession of the earth* (verse 9), but they even *lay clai to heaven* (verse 9). Added to their immunity to trouble an their arrogant ways is their popularity with the world (vers 10,11). The people ask why God, if indeed He knows abor them, does not punish them (verse 11).

The psalmist concludes his description of the wicke *always carefree, they increase in wealth.* Then he cries out bi terly: *Surely in vain have I kept my heart pure* (verse 13), f while the wicked flourish, *all day long I have been plague* (verse 14). If the wicked prosper, it is vain to be righteou Righteousness does not pay; the big dividends go to th wicked.

Surely God is good to Israel,
to those who are pure in heart.

²But as for me, my feet had almost slipped;
I had nearly lost my foothold.

³For I envied the arrogant
when I saw the prosperity of the wicked.

⁴They have no struggles;
their bodies are healthy and strong.

⁵They are free from the burdens common to man;
they are not plagued by human ills.

⁶Therefore pride is their necklace;
they clothe themselves with violence.

⁷From their callous hearts comes iniquity;
the evil conceits of their minds know no limits.

⁸They scoff, and speak with malice;
in their arrogance they threaten oppression.

⁹Their mouths lay claim to heaven,
and their tongues take possession of the earth.

¹⁰Therefore their people turn to them
and drink up waters in abundance.

¹¹They say, "How can God know?
Does the Most High have knowledge?"

¹²This is what the wicked are like –
always carefree, they increase in wealth.

¹³Surely in vain have I kept my heart pure;
in vain have I washed my hands in innocence.

¹⁴All day long I have been plagued;
I have been punished every morning.

¹⁵If I had said, "I will speak thus,"
I would have betrayed your children.

¹⁶When I tried to understand all this,
it was oppressive to me

¹⁷till I entered the sanctuary of God;
then I understood their final destiny.

¹⁸Surely you place them on slippery ground;
you cast them down to ruin.

¹⁹How suddenly are they destroyed,
completely swept away by terrors!

²⁰As a dream when one awakes,
so when you arise, O Lord,
you will despise them as fantasies.

²¹When my heart was grieved
and my spirit embittered,

²²I was senseless and ignorant;
I was a brute beast before you.

²³Yet I am always with you;
you hold me by my right hand.

²⁴You guide me with your counsel,
and afterwards you will take me into glory.

²⁵Whom have I in heaven but you?
And earth has nothing I desire besides you.

²⁶My flesh and my heart may fail,
but God is the strength of my heart
and my portion for ever.

²⁷Those who are far from you will perish;
you destroy all who are unfaithful to you.

²⁸But as for me, it is good to be near God.
I have made the Sovereign LORD my refuge;
I will tell of all your deeds.

The right approach to the problem (verses 15,16)

The reason why the psalmist so nearly stumbled and fell (verse 2) is that his approach was wrong. He made at least three mistakes. First, he *envied* the wicked (verse 3). But it is always wrong to envy the sinner's liberty to sin. "Do not let your heart envy sinners, but always be zealous for the fear of the LORD" (Proverbs 23:17). Secondly, he became bitter against God, as he later confesses (verses 21-22). To make presumptuous complaints against God is to behave like an ignorant animal, not like a rational human being. Thirdly, he was tempted to give up. When he tried to understand, he says, *it was oppressive to me* (verse 16). He could find no solution and was inclined to give in to despair.

But perplexity and hopelessness lasted only *till I entered the sanctuary of God* (verse 17). Perception is granted to those who humbly seek God's face. The Christian in the twentieth century needs to learn this lesson. When we are perplexed by the problems of God's providential rule in the world, we are neither to look at the wicked with envy nor at ourselves in bitter self-pity. Nor should we give up looking for any solution and lapse into despair, but rather fall on our knees and look at God. Then "from the secret place of the Most High we see things as God sees them" (Campbell Morgan).

The solution (verses 17-27)

Our problems are aggravated because we are narrow-minded and short-sighted. It is a question of perspective. A mountain which appears menacing when we stand at its foot and towers above us, shrinks into harmless insignificance when we view it from a distance or from the air. So the problem of God's providence cannot be solved in the limited context of time and earth; its solution awaits the next world and eternity. Many of life's inequalities will remain now. But wrongs will be righted, evil avenged, and good vindicated in the final judgment. This is why we need to keep going into *the sanctuary of God*; it is there that our perspective is adjusted and our vision clarified.

What the psalmist was able in God's sanctuary to grasp was the *final destiny* of these people (verse 17). They flourish now it is true, but God sets them *on slippery ground*. In the words of Jesus, they are on "the broad road that leads to destruction." Ultimately death will claim them and they will be *destroyed*. Indeed, *as a dream when one awakes*, the very memory of them will vanish away (verses 17-19).

If that is the fate of the wicked, very different is the destiny of the righteous: *I am always with you* (verse 23). That is though the ungodly flourish now, only to perish in the end, the godly enjoy the presence of God perpetually, both now and forever (verse 24). God's people may suffer want and persecution, but their abiding wealth is in God Himself. In one of the sublimest expressions of personal religion in the Old Testament the psalmist continues: *Whom have I in heaven but you? And earth has nothing I desire besides you* (verse 25). In heaven and earth, in time and eternity, the living God is his *portion for ever* (verse 26). Such communion with God is eternal life; death can neither disturb nor destroy it.

In conclusion, verses 27 and 28 summarise the contrasting destinies of the godly and the ungodly which the psalmist perceived in the sanctuary of God: *Those who are far from you will perish... but as for me, it is good to be near God.* No doubt nearness to God does not appear "good" to the materialist since it may involve sorrow and suffering in the world. But those who prize true riches know that our real and eternal "good" is in God.

72

Psalm 84

The Courts of the Lord

The Temple in Jerusalem was for the Jew the most sacred spot on earth, for there in the Holy of Holies was the Shekinah glory, the visible manifestation of the presence of God. Of course the pious Israelite knew perfectly well, as Solomon had said, that God does not "dwell on earth" and that "the heaven, even the highest heaven cannot contain" Him (1 Kings 8:27). Nevertheless, He had been pleased to "put his name" in Jerusalem and to cause the symbol of His presence to appear upon the mercy-seat behind the veil of the Temple. As a result, every Israelite loved the Temple and looked forward eagerly to every chance to visit it, especially on the three annual festivals. He could sincerely sing: *How lovely is your dwelling-place, O LORD Almighty* (verse 1). The same longing for the Temple is found in Psalms 42 and 43 and in some of the pilgrim psalms (120-134).

The blessedness of others (verses 1-7)
The psalmist begins by expressing how desirable God's dwelling-place is to Him. His whole being longs for it, *soul, heart,* and *flesh*. He *yearns, even faints* for it, because to enter *the courts of the LORD* is equivalent to approaching *the living God* Himself. But for some reason he is prevented from fulfilling his heart's desire. So he looks with envy upon those, both birds and humans, who can enjoy what at present is denied to him.

How lovely is your dwelling-place,
    O LORD Almighty!
My soul yearns, even faints
    for the courts of the LORD;
my heart and my flesh cry out
    for the living God.

Even the sparrow has found a home,
    and the swallow a nest for herself,
    where she may have her young –
a place near your altar,
    O LORD Almighty, my King and my God.

Blessed are those who dwell in your house;
    they are ever praising you.   *Selah*

⁵Blessed are those whose strength is in you,
    who have set their hearts on pilgrimage.
⁶As they pass through the Valley of Baca,
    they make it a place of springs;
    the autumn rains also cover it with pools.
⁷They go from strength to strength
    till each appears before God in Zion.

⁸Hear my prayer, O LORD God Almighty;
    listen to me, O God of Jacob. *Selah*
⁹Look upon our shield, O God;
    look with favour on your anointed one.

¹⁰Better is one day in your courts
    than a thousand elsewhere;
I would rather be a doorkeeper in the house of my God
    than dwell in the tents of the wicked.
¹¹For the LORD God is a sun and shield;
    the LORD bestows favour and honour;
no good thing does he withhold
    from those whose walk is blameless.

¹²O LORD Almighty,
    blessed is the man who trusts in you.

He thinks of the sparrows, the most numerous and commor
birds in the world, constructing their nests in every availab
nook and cranny of the Temple buildings. The *swallow*
probably the swift. Large numbers still visit Palestine on mi
ration, and many nest even today in the precincts of the Mc
que of Omar in Jerusalem. How fortunate these birds seem
the psalmist! They are permitted to dwell in the immedia
proximity of the altars of God. Chattering sparrows ar
screaming swifts appear to unite with the people of God
they worship him. To them the writer now turns, the pries
who *dwell* in God's house, always praising him (verse 4), ar
the pilgrims who visit it from time to time. He pronounc
them both *blessed* (verses 4,5).

He concentrates on the pilgrims (verses 5-7), no dou
because he longs to be one himself, and gives a graphic descri
tion of their journey up to Jerusalem. They *have set their hear
on pilgrimage* (verse 5), and their resolute purpose strengthe
them on their arduous trek. He pictures them passing throu
an arid valley (*the Valley of Baca*). But even such forbiddir
parts of the journey do not deter the pilgrims. On the contrar
they find there *a place of springs* for *the autumn rains al
cover it with pools*. In other words, "hope sustains them
every step" (Bishop Perowne). They go *from strength
strength*, fortified by the joyful expectation of appearir
before God in Zion (verse 7).

A personal prayer (verses 8-12)
As the psalmist describes the blessedness of sparrows ar
swifts, pilgrims and priests, who visit the Temple or dwe
there, his own longing to join them breaks out into a prayer:
LORD *God Almighty, listen to me...* (verse 8). There follows
prayer for God's *anointed one* (verse 9), which must mean t
king. We can only guess its relevance in this context. Perhap
it is that the nation's welfare was bound up in the king's.

The writer goes on to indicate the reason for his prayer
visit the Temple, and expresses it forcefully in terms of bo
time and space (verse 10). One day in the courts of the Lord, I
says, is to him better *than a thousand elsewhere*, while to be
mere *doorkeeper in the house of my God*, approaching on
the threshold of the Temple, was preferable to dwelling at eas
in the tents of the wicked. Only a day. Only a doorkeeper. Ar
yet such a fleeting and distant contact with God would be sati
fying, since He is a *sun*, bathing us with light, *and shiel
defending us from evil. More than that, He gives *favour an
honour*; in fact *no good thing does he withhold from tho.
whose walk is blameless* (verse 11).

The psalm ends with another statement of who is *blessed.
is not only the priests who dwell in the Temple precincts (vers

4) and the pilgrims who visit them (verse 5), but all people w[ho]
put their trust in God (verse 12), whether or not they have t[he]
opportunity to go up to Jerusalem.

Christian worshipers have no difficulty in applying th[e]
psalm to themselves, for the New Testament tells us plai[n]
what the temple of God is which we may call *lovely* and ma[ke]
the object of our desire. First, it is the church, not only univ[er]
sal (Ephesians 2:21) but local (1 Corinthians 3:16; 2 Corin[th]
ians 6:16), that is, every company of believers. God does n[ot]
dwell in temples made with hands (Acts 7:48) but among H[is]
people. We do not need to travel to Jerusalem to meet Hi[m.]
When only two or three of us have met in the name of Chri[st]
He is there in our midst (Matthew 18:20). This is why we lo[ve]
to come together for public worship.

But the final fulfilment of the temple idea will be heaven, t[he]
new Jerusalem, of which it is written: "I did not see a temple [in]
the city, because the Lord God Almighty and the Lamb are [its]
temple," and "Now the dwelling of God is with men, and [he]
will live with them. They will be his people, and God hims[elf]
will be with them and be their God" (Revelation 21:22,3). [In]
this sense, too, Christian believers know in their own expe[ri]
ence the psalmist's ardent longing for the temple of God. [We]
thirst for God, and our Christian hope sustains us on o[ur]
weary pilgrimage to heaven.

In his paraphrase of this psalm, Henry Francis Lyte skilfu[lly]
combines the double New Testament application of the temp[le]
theme to Christian worship and to heaven:

Pleasant are your courts above,
In the land of light and love;
Pleasant are your courts below,
In this land of sin and woe.
Oh! my spirit longs and faints
For the converse of your saints,
For the brightness of your face,
For your fulness, God of grace.

Psalm 90

Life's Transient Dream

This psalm sets out the brevity of human existence in the light of God's eternity. The author refers to some period of special affliction (verse 15) as well as to humankind's universal frailty and sinfulness. Yet he betrays no sign of despair or complaint; his spirit is one of humble submission and trust.

God's eternity (verses 1-6)

The psalm opens with a magnificent statement of the eternity of God, because of which He has ever been the *dwelling-place* of His people. The word for *dwelling-place* is the same as that in Deuteronomy 33:27: "The eternal God is your *refuge*, and underneath are the everlasting arms." Amid all the ups and downs of life our only security is in Him who, before the birth of the mountains and creation of the earth, indeed *from everlasting to everlasting*, is God.

Human beings are by contrast creatures of dust. In a clear allusion to Genesis 3:19, God is described as commanding them to return to dust (verse 3). Such is the reality of death, "earth to earth, ashes to ashes, dust to dust." We are not only mortal, but extremely short-lived. To God a whole millennium is equivalent to a day (compare 2 Peter 3:8) or even to one of the watches of the night (verse 4). But in comparison with the

Lord, you have been our dwelling-place
throughout all generations.
Before the mountains were born
or you brought forth the earth and the world,
from everlasting to everlasting you are God.

You turn men back to dust,
saying, "Return to dust, O sons of men."
For a thousand years in your sight
are like a day that has just gone by,
or like a watch in the night.
You sweep men away in the sleep of death;
they are like the new grass of the morning –
though in the morning it springs up new,
by evening it is dry and withered.

[7]We are consumed by your anger
and terrified by your indignation.
[8]You have set our iniquities before you,
our secret sins in the light of your presence.
[9]All our days pass away under your wrath;
we finish our years with a moan.
[10]The length of our days is seventy years –
or eighty, if we have the strength;
yet their span is but trouble and sorrow,
for they quickly pass, and we fly away.
[11]Who knows the power of your anger?
For your wrath is as great as the fear that is due you.
[12]Teach us to number our days aright,
that we may gain a heart of wisdom.

[13]Relent, O LORD! How long will it be?
Have compassion on your servants.

[14]Satisfy us in the morning with your unfailing love,
that we may sing for joy and be glad all our days.
[15]Make us glad for as many days as you have afflicted us,
for as many years as we have seen trouble.

[16]May your deeds be shown to your servants,
your splendour to their children.

[17]May the favour of the Lord our God rest upon us;
establish the work of our hands for us –
yes, establish the work of our hands.

divine timelessness, our human life is *like the new grass*, whi[ch] flourishes in the morning but is withered by the eveni[ng] scorched by sun and wind. This is a constant theme of Scr[ip]ture, and other vivid metaphors are used to stress the brevity [of] our life on earth. It is like water spilt on the ground, like [a] shadow which passes when the sun comes out, and like smo[ke] or mist dispersed by the wind.

God's wrath (verses 7-11)

In the next paragraph the thought moves on from God's et[er]nity to His wrath. At first it may seem an abrupt transition, b[ut] the psalmist sees human mortality against the da[rk] background of God's displeasure at sin. This is not only t[hat] the nation was passing through some calamity which he att[ri]butes to the judgment of God, but because he recognises t[hat] death is the penalty for human sin (Genesis 2:17; 3:1[9]; Romans 5:12). So he writes of our *iniquities* and even *our s[ec]ret sins* being open before God (verse 8), and says that *all o[ur] days pass away under your wrath* (verse 9). Our average sp[an] of life may be seventy years, yet even these are *trouble and s[or]row*. This is not said in bitterness, but in calm and so[ber] realism. Every human being is destined to die, and our brief l[ife] span is spent under the judgment of God (verse 11), unless a[nd] until we find mercy. This brings us naturally to the pray[er] with which the psalm concludes.

God's mercy (verses 12-17)

The first prayer inspired by a sense of human sin and mortal[ity] is in verse 12: *Teach us to number our days aright, that we m[ay] gain a heart of wisdom. Wisdom* consists of knowing and fe[ar]ing God; life is so short that it is folly to ignore Him. The ri[ch] farmer in the parable of Jesus, who planned and spoke as if [life] lasted for ever, God called a fool.

Secondly, *Satisfy us in the morning with your unfailing lo[ve]* for if we find our peace in the love of God early, we shall [be] *glad all our days* (verses 13,14). Further, the joy God gives will make up for the years of adversity (verse 15).

The third prayer is concerned with our *work*. One of t[he] tragedies of death is that it interrupts our labor and cuts sh[ort] our achievement. This is true, however, only of hum[an] endeavor undertaken in human strength. When God shows [his] *work* to His servants, manifesting his power on their beh[alf] and blessing them with His favor, the result is that He prosp[ers] *the work of our hands for us* (verses 16,17). The only wo[rk] which lasts is that which God establishes.

The brevity of life should still constrain us to get a heart [of] wisdom, namely to make God our refuge, to find rest in H[is] love and fruitful labor under His blessing.

Psalm 91

The Defence of the Most High

This psalm has an unusual distinction: it is the only passage Scripture which (at least in the sacred record) is quoted by devil! (See Matthew 4:6 and Luke 4:10,11.) This is m important than it sounds, because actually the devil misquo it, or rather misapplied it. He urged the Son of God to thr Himself down from the pinnacle of the Temple and trust Gc promise (verses 11 and 12) that His angels would protect H so that He would not hurt Himself. The devil is not the o person who has attempted to misapply Psalm 91, as if it prc ised an unconditional security in any and every circumstar

Our Lord knew, however, that to jump from the roof of Temple on the basis of this psalm's promise of divine pro tion would be to tempt God. Only children of God who are ing in the will of God can expect the protection of God. E then, they have no guarantee of being shielded from all h: (see verse 15). What they know is that ultimately, whate their circumstances may be, they are secure in God's lc Psalm 91 is, in fact, the Old Testament equivalent of Rom 8:31-39.

The best way to grasp the sequence of thought is to see t first the believer speaks to God (verses 1,2); then the psaln addresses the believer (verses 3-13); while finally God in venes, speaking to the reader, and Himself confirms believer's assurance of security which is the theme of the ps: (verses 14-16).

¹He who dwells in the shelter of the
  Most High
will rest in the shadow of the
  Almighty.
²I will say of the LORD, "He is my refuge
  and my fortress,
my God, in whom I trust."

³Surely he will save you from the
  fowler's snare
and from the deadly pestilence.
⁴He will cover you with feathers,
  and under his wings you will find
  refuge;
his faithfulness will be your shield
  and rampart.
⁵You will not fear the terror of night,
  nor the arrow that flies by day,

⁶nor the pestilence that stalks in the
  darkness,
nor the plague that destroys at
  midday.
⁷A thousand may fall at your side,
  ten thousand at your right hand,
but it will not come near you.
⁸You will only observe with your eyes
  and see the punishment of the
  wicked.

⁹If you make the Most High your
  dwelling –
even the LORD, who is my refuge –
¹⁰then no harm will befall you,
  no disaster will come near your tent.
¹¹For he will command his angels
  concerning you
to guard you in all your ways;

¹²they will lift you up in their hands,
  so that you will not strike your foot
  against a stone.
¹³You will tread upon the lion and the
  cobra;
you will trample the great lion and
  the serpent.

¹⁴"Because he loves me," says the
  LORD, "I will rescue him;
I will protect him, for he
  acknowledges my name.
¹⁵He will call upon me, and I will answe
  him;
I will be with him in trouble,
  I will deliver him and honour him.
¹⁶With long life will I satisfy him
  and show him my salvation."

The believer (verses 1,2)

The believer's faith is grounded upon who God is. He is *the Most High* and *the Almighty* on the one hand (verse 1), infinite in transcendence and power; but on the other he is *the* L*ORD* (verse 2), Yahweh, the covenant God of Israel, bound to His people by a solemn undertaking. To *rest in the shadow* of such a God is wisdom; He is the believer's *refuge* and *fortress*.

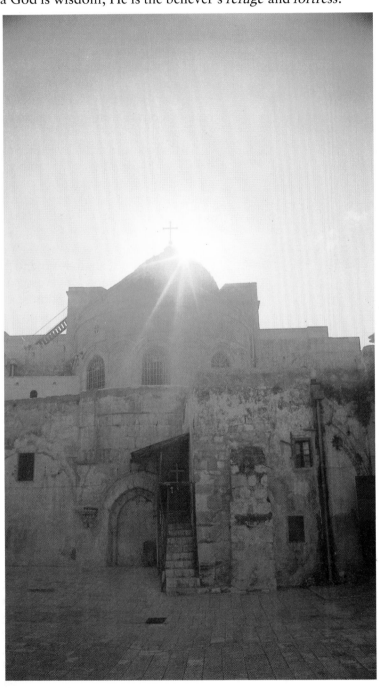

e Church of the Holy
ulchre, Jerusalem. This
ch-visited church is
ieved to be built over
 site of Golgotha,
ere Jesus was crucified.
 you make the Most
gh your dwelling... then
 harm will befall you."

The psalmist (verses 3-13)

Having quoted this confession of faith, the psalmist nc
endorses it, encouraging believers in it and assuring them
their safety. Bold imagery is used to illustrate the divi
defence which is promised. God will defend them as a moth
bird hides her chicks under her wings; His *faithfulness* will
to them as a soldier's *shield* (verse 4). What, then, are the per
from which believers will be delivered? They are various
described: *the fowler's snare... the deadly pestilence* (verse .
the terror of night... the arrow... by day (verse 5), *the pestilen*
and the plague (verse 6).

It is perfectly possible to interpret this figurative language
referring to literal calamities. But some writers suggest th
real demons are in view, derived perhaps from Babyloni.
sources.

Be that as it may, deliverance is plainly promised from a
evil. *Ten thousand* may succumb to it (verse 7), and the *wick*
shall reap the *punishment* of their sins (verse 8), but to tho
who make the Lord their refuge, it may be confiden
asserted: *no harm will befall you* (verses 9,10). God's ange
will protect them (verses 11,12; compare Psalm 34:7 and He
rews 1:14), so that not even the *lion and the cobra... and t*
serpent (verse 13) shall be able to harm them. The snake is t
subtlest and the lion the strongest of all creatures. It is n
without significance that Satan is called "that ancient serpen
and depicted as prowling round "like a roaring lion" (Revel
tion 12:9; 20:1 and 1 Peter 5:8).

The Lord (verses 14-16)

Finally, the Lord himself is heard to speak, neither to t
believer nor to the psalmist, but to the reader, approving t
believer's faith and the psalmist's theme. Has the psalm
affirmed: *he will save you*? He is quite right. Twice God echo
the same words Himself: *I will rescue... I will deliver* (vers
14,15). Why? *Because he loves me.* God is the supreme obje
of the believer's love as well as faith, and it is to those who lo
God that the assurance is given that "in all things God wor
for their good" (Romans 8:28). Not that believers can affo
to be idle and do nothing. They must trust God, and expre
their faith in prayer. Then God *will* answer them. The divi
deliverance does not, however, always mean an escape fro
trouble; it sometimes means finding God with them *in troub*
(verse 15). The final promise which God makes to His trusti
servants is of *long life* and *salvation* (verse 16). It is not impc
sible that, like the prophets, the psalmist wrote more than
knew, for the ultimate meaning of security is that eternal li
and salvation which are found in Jesus Christ alone.

Psalm 95

An Invitation to Sing and to Hear

This psalm is a summons to the people of God, who know Him as the *Rock* of their salvation (verse 1), both to sing His praises and to hear His word. From at least as early as the fourth century A.D. it has been sung in many churches at the beginning of public worship.

An invitation to sing God's praise (verses 1-7)
In King Henry VIII's devotional primer, Psalm 95 is called "a song stirring to the praise of God." And what a stirring summons it is! In verses 1, 2, and 6 there are seven exhortations one after the other. Indeed, members of the congregation, no doubt gathered in the Temple courts, are represented as engaged in mutual exhortation. They are inciting one another to worship and urging each other to sing the praises of God, since public worship is essentially congregational.

In this psalm we are given incentives as well as invitations to worship. We do not just hear the repetitive *let us*, but the added *for the LORD is...* giving us a reason for our praise. Not until we grasp who the Lord is, are we inwardly moved to worship Him.

Who, then, is He? The answer of this canticle is that He is both *the great God* (verse 3) and *our God* (verse 7).

First, He is *the great God.* He is supreme in heaven (verse 3), *the great King above all gods.* There is no need to assume that the psalmist credited them with an objective reality, for "all the

¹Come, let us sing for joy to the LORD;
   let us shout aloud to the Rock of our
      salvation.
²Let us come before him with
      thanksgiving
   and extol him with music and song.

³For the LORD is the great God,
   the great King above all gods.
⁴In his hand are the depths of the earth,
   and the mountain peaks belong to
      him.
⁵The sea is his, for he made it,
   and his hands formed the dry land.

⁶Come, let us bow down in worship,
   let us kneel before the LORD our
      Maker,

⁷for he is our God
   and we are the people of his pasture,
      the flock under his care.

   Today, if you hear his voice,
⁸do not harden your hearts as you did at
      Meribah,
   as you did that day at Massah in the
      desert,
⁹where your fathers tested and tried me,
   though they had seen what I did.
¹⁰For forty years I was angry with that
      generation;
   I said, "They are a people whose
      hearts go astray,
   and they have not known my ways."
¹¹So I declared on oath in my anger,
   "They shall never enter my rest."

A squall on the Sea of Galilee. "The sea is his, for he made it, and his hands formed the dry land."

gods of the nations are idols" (Psalm 96:5). God is also supreme on earth (verses 4,5). Every dimension is included, in order to show that nothing is beyond the dominion of God. The depths of the earth, the heights of the mountains, and the broad expanses of sea and land are all His. They are in his hand (verse 4), because his hands formed them (verse 5). The hand that made the universe in the beginning still holds the universe today. God is the controller of the natural order because He was the creator of it.

Secondly, he is our God (verse 7). Far above us in His greatness, He is yet close to us in His goodness. His majesty is tempered with mercy, and his glory with grace. Did He make the world? He made Israel, too. He is the LORD our Maker (verse 6; see also Psalms 100:3; 149:2; Isaiah 51:13; 54:5). The Creator of all things is the Redeemer of His special people. He is our Shepherd as well, calling us the people of his pasture (verse 7).

Psalm 95 makes it plain that our mood will change in worship according to which aspect of God is occupying our attention. In verses 1 and 2 the invitation is to make a joyful noise to the Lord and come into His presence with thanksgiving, *for the LORD is a great God*. Because of his greatness in creation, we may well shout aloud in jubilation. But in verse 6 the invitation is to *kneel before the LORD*. Why? *For he is our God* (verse 7). Has this great God condescended to be our God, becoming our shepherd and calling us His sheep? Then this is no moment for exuberant hilarity, but rather for awe and wonder, as with bated breath we prostrate ourselves before Him in reverence and humility.

With the end of verse 7 the mood changes again. The speaker changes too. So far the congregation have been exhorting one another; now God intervenes and speaks to His people Himself.

An invitation to hear God's word (verses 8-11)

We are not only to open our lips to sing God's praise, but t open our ears to hear His word. It is noteworthy that tho who are exhorted to hear God's voice have been described the previous verse as *the flock under his care*, because of cour a sheep should know the shepherd's voice. Compare Joh 10:2-4.

The early days of Israel are taken by God as a striking obje lesson. A month or two after the Exodus, just before the reached Mount Sinai, the children of Israel camped Rephidim. There was no water. So the people found fault wit Moses: "Give us water to drink. Why did you bring us out Egypt to kill us, our children and cattle with thirst?" Mos prayed to the Lord, and at His instruction struck the rock wit the rod of God, and water gushed out. Moses then gave to th place two names, *Massah* meaning testing or temptation, ar *Meribah* meaning quarrelling or provocation. This story recorded in Exodus 17:1-7.

Forty years later a similar crisis arose at Kadesh. Water w again miraculously provided for the people, when they con plained to Moses. This place came to be known as *Meriba Kadesh*, to distinguish it from the *Meribah* at Rephidim. Th second story is recorded in Numbers 20:1-13.

God's people had tested their God. They had put Him to tl proof. Although they had seen His works, they had no faith Him. God had wonderfully rescued them from their bonda; in Egypt. He later established His covenant with them, gav them His special revelation, and provided for them in the wi derness. Yet here they were rebelling against Him, and doub ing His love and goodness. No wonder we go on to read, *for years I was angry with that generation*. God also describe them as *a people whose hearts go astray* (verse 10). Their wa dering in the wilderness was an outward counterpart to the straying hearts. So great was Israel's sin, unbelief, and rebel ion, that it aroused a feeling of revulsion in the heart and mir of God (verse 11). God is revealed in Scripture as a God of lo and wrath, of goodness and severity. He hates sin with a implacable hatred, while yet loving the sinner with an inexti guishable love.

The letter to the Hebrews makes these verses an urgent me sage for Christians today. "So the Holy Spirit says: 'Today, you hear his voice, do not harden your hearts as you did in t rebellion, during the time of testing in the desert...'" (Hebrev 3:7,8). It is today which is the day of salvation; we mu beware lest we become "hardened by sin's deceitfulness (Hebrews 3:13).

Psalm 98

Jehovah, the Savior-King

The occasion of this psalm is evidently some great national victory, which has been achieved by God's right hand and holy arm, and in the sight of the nations. Whether the divine victory was over Egypt or Babylon or some other foe, it certainly foreshadows that mightier salvation from sin, Satan and death, which God has brought to us through Jesus Christ His Son. This is the most marvellous of the *marvellous things* (verse 1) which God has done, and it prompts the people of God to keep singing a *new song*, new from ever fresh wonder at His grace. Christian songs of praise are fundamentally a rejoicing in the *marvellous things* which God has done.

The psalmist's call to praise is not only due to God's mighty acts of the past. He sees them also as evidence of the present reign of God, and as a pledge that He will set up His final kingdom of righteousness on earth. His threefold theme, therefore, concerns God the Savior, the King and the Judge. He invites God's people to sing to Him as their Savior (verses 1-4), *all the earth* (verse 4) to worship Him as King (verses 4-6), and nature (sea, the world, rivers and mountains) to do homage to Him as the coming Judge (verses 7-9).

God the Savior (verses 1-3)
The victory of God which inspired the composition of this psalm was gained by Himself alone. He had no human co-operation. He relied upon *his right hand and his holy arm*

¹Sing to the LORD a new song,
  for he has done marvellous things;
his right hand and his holy arm
  have worked salvation for him.
²The LORD has made his salvation known
  and revealed his righteousness to the nations.
³He has remembered his love
  and his faithfulness to the house of Israel;
all the ends of the earth have seen
  the salvation of our God.

⁴Shout for joy to the LORD, all the earth,
  burst into jubilant song with music;
⁵make music to the LORD with the harp,
  with the harp and the sound of singing,

⁶with trumpets and the blast of the ram's horn –
  shout for joy before the LORD, the King.

⁷Let the sea resound, and all that is in it,
  the world, and all who live in it.
⁸Let the rivers clap their hands,
  let the mountains sing together for joy;
⁹let them sing before the LORD,
  for he comes to judge the earth.
He will judge the world in righteousness
  and the peoples with equity.

A young Jewish boy reads from the Law at his Barmitzvah ceremony in front of the Western Wall, Jerusalem.

(verse 1). Since "God is spirit" (John 4:24), he has no body, c course, and therefore neither hands nor arms. Nevertheles these vivid anthropomorphic expressions symbolise both H strength and His direct intervention on behalf of His peopl The redemption from Egypt and from Babylon are alil ascribed in Scripture to the strong arm or mighty hand of Go (see for example Exodus 15:6,12; Psalm 44:1-3; and Isaia 52:10; 59:16; 63:5).

Further, this victory of God was no secret affair, but rathe a public spectacle. He *revealed* it in the sight of the natior (verse 2). What they saw was His *salvation* and His *righteou ness.*

God had also made known His *love and his faithfulness the house of Israel* (verse 4). Israel were God's chosen peopl with whom He had entered into a solemn covenant. Th covenant He would never break, nor forget. Indeed, the recer deliverance was a proof of His loyalty to it. So Israel coul praise God not only for His power, which gained the victor but for His faithfulness out of which it sprang. Although it w: a victory gained for Israel by Israel's God, (*our God*), it ha been seen by *all the ends of the earth* in fulfilment of tl prophecy of Isaiah 52:10, which John the Baptist applied the salvation of Jesus (Luke 3:6). The combination of *love* an *faithfulness* may also be seen throughout Psalm 89, in Psaln 92:2 and 100:5, and Micah 7:20.

God the King (verses 4-6)
If the people of Israel have been summoned to praise God, now are the inhabitants of *all the earth* (verse 4; compa Psalm 100:1). Even if they have not like Israel experienced H salvation, they can with Israel recognise His kingdom. He *the LORD, the King* (verse 6). His mighty deliverance of H people is a visible token of His sovereign rule over the affai of human beings and nations. He is to be worshiped not mere with a *shout* (verse 4), but with singing and musical instr ments (verse 5,6).

It seems likely that these outward expressions of rejoicir are chosen because they commonly accompanied the accessic or coronation of a new king. When Zadok anointed Solomc king, they blew the trumpet, and the people shouted ar rejoiced with music (1 Kings 1:39,40). Similarly, when the bc king Joash was crowned and anointed by Jehoiada the pries there was a clapping of hands as well (2 Kings 11:12-14). the reign of Jehovah is to be similarly celebrated with singir and shouting, with clapping of hands and blowing of trumpe (compare Psalm 47). There was in Hebrew worship wh C.S.Lewis calls a certain "gusto."

Part of the Good Friday procession of Christian pilgrims along the *Via Dolorosa*, in the old city of Jerusalem.

God the Judge (verses 7-9)

In this worship of men and women, expressed jubilant through musical instruments and the human voice, the who range of animate and inanimate nature is now invited to joi The sea and its denizens, the world and its inhabitants, t floods and the hills are together to be joyful *before the Lo* (verses 6,9). The roaring of the sea is its worship; in the splas ing of the floods we can hear them clap their hands. The reaso for their rejoicing lies yet in the future.

It seems to be recognised that nature is subject to some kir of bondage, as the apostle Paul was later to show in Roma 8:18-25, and it would be delivered only when God came to s up His kingdom. He is already King (verse 6), but the ear does not yet acknowledge His rule. So He is coming to jud the earth, and its peoples (verse 9). Only when God's rule established on earth (as it has begun to be through Chris although the Messianic kingdom is pictured in this psalm as rule of Jehovah Himself), will the peoples and nature itself l subdued and righteously governed. He who has already show His righteousness in the saving of His people (verse 2), w exhibit it again in His judging of the world. This judgment w include the punishment of the wicked, as is made plain Isaiah 11:1-5. But even in this too we may rejoice, for we sha recognise that "true and just are his judgments," and concu ring in them we shall cry, "Amen, Hallelujah!" (Revelatic 19:1-5).

Psalm 100

The Lord is God and Good

This psalm was sung by the Israelites first in the Temple, and then in the daily synagogue services. The medieval church sang it in the service called Lauds. It is most popular today in its metrical version, "All people that on earth do dwell," which was probably composed by William Kethe, a sixteenth-century Scotsman and friend of the Reformer John Knox.

It has only five verses, but it is an eloquent summons to worship; and the worship to which it bids us is to have two marks.

Two characteristics of worship

This psalm is often called "the Jubilate", which means "O be joyful!" or "shout aloud!". Joy is to characterise our worship. Psalm 100 is one of a group of eight which celebrate the kingly sovereignty of Jehovah. "The LORD reigns, he is robed in majesty... Your throne was established long ago." "The LORD is the great God, the great King above all gods." "Say among the nations: 'The LORD reigns.'" "The LORD reigns, let the earth be glad." "Shout for joy before the LORD, the King." "The LORD reigns, let the nations tremble." (Psalms 93:1,2; 95:3; 96:10; 97:1; 98:6; 99:1). Of these royal psalms the hundredth is the doxology.

For if God is king, what can our worship be but joyful? Away with funereal faces and doleful dirges! Joy, gladness, and singing are to be the accompaniment of worship.

> ¹Shout for joy to the LORD, all the earth,
> ² Serve the LORD with gladness;
>   come before him with joyful songs.
> ³Know that the LORD is God.
>   It is he who made us, and we are his;
>   we are his people, the sheep of his
>   pasture.
>
> ⁴Enter his gates with thanksgiving
>   and his courts with praise;
>   give thanks to him and praise his
>   name.
> ⁵For the LORD is good and his love
>   endures for ever;
>   his faithfulness continues through all
>   generations.

The Golden Gate, Jerusalem, looks out across the Kidron Valley. Both Jews and Moslems believe that this will be the site of the Last Judgment.

Our worship is to be universal as well as joyful. *Shout for jo[y] all the earth* (verse 1). It is true that this psalm concer[ns] Jehovah, the God of Israel; but the psalmist realises that He [is] not Israel's monopoly. Had He not sworn to Abraham: "[In] your seed shall all the families of the earth be blessed"? Is it n[ot] written in Isaiah 56:6,7: "And foreigners who bind themselv[es] to the LORD to serve him, to love the name of the LORD... the[m] will I bring to my holy mountain and give them joy in my hou[se] of prayer... for my house will be called a house of prayer for [all] nations."? Then no nation should stand aside from this call [to] worship. Jehovah is not the tribal deity of Israel, but th[e] sovereign Ruler over all the earth. When we assemble for wo[r-] ship, therefore, we should desire not only to make a joyf[ul] noise ourselves, but that all nations should unite with us in o[ur] joyful task.

The rest of this psalm is devoted to an exposition of why t[he] nations should join us. Worship is not only to be joyful a[nd] universal, but reasonable.

The greatness of God

Know that the LORD is God (verse 3). How we worship depends on what we know. Knowledge and understanding play an important part in our worship. Christians do not worship "an unknown God," like the ancient Athenians, but a God who has revealed Himself.

What then are we to know? The gods of the heathen are idols; they can neither see, nor speak, nor act. Our God is a living and active God. Moreover, the chief evidence which the psalmist gives of His activity is to be found in the history of Israel. He redeemed His people from their bondage in Egypt, entered into a covenant with them at Mount Sinai, led them across the wilderness, and settled them in the Promised Land. In a word He *made* them (compare Deuteronomy 32:6,15 and Psalm 95:6). *It is he who made us, and we are his* (verse 3). Of this sovereign, intervening activity of God, two vivid illustrations are given.

First, God is the potter. *It is he who made us.* God is here likened to a craftsman. It is not the individual, but the nation to which the phrase refers. Israel is sometimes called by God in the Old Testament "the work of my hands" (see for example Isaiah 29:23; 60:21).

With what immense skill and patience did the divine potter pursue His labor! His raw material was always unpromising and often recalcitrant. Others would have long since abandoned all hope of success. But He persevered. Undeterred by any setback, and refusing to be discouraged by any disappointment, He went on fashioning Israel into a vessel of honor, for His own use.

Secondly, God is the shepherd. *We are his people, the sheep of his pasture.* The potter who made them was the shepherd who tended them. Through all the vicissitudes of their colorful career, He protected and guided them. He watched over them with all the conscientious tenderness of an eastern shepherd.

So it is with us also. God has redeemed us and brought us to Himself. We can say that He is our potter and our shepherd. Nothing could indicate more clearly and emphatically than this what we owe to the sovereign grace of God. It is He who has made us and we are His people. We have neither created nor constituted ourselves the people of God. "By the grace of God we are what we are." What we are is therefore cause for praise, not for pride.

No wonder the psalmist bursts into another call to worship: *Enter his gates with thanksgiving and his courts with praise; give thanks to him and praise his name* (verse 4). Our worship is to be joyful simply because it is grateful.

The goodness of God
The Lord is not only great, but *good* (verse 5). There is ground to praise Him not only for what He has done, but for what He is.

Wherein does His goodness consist? It consists in His love which *endures for ever* and His *faithfulness* (verse 5). Our God is a covenant-keeping God. He is neither fickle nor faithless. His word is dependable, and His promises are trustworthy. From generation to generation He remains the same. From everlasting to everlasting He is God.

We are summoned to worship Him not just because He has made us and taken us to Himself to be His own, but because He will stay by us. The heavenly potter will never discard His work; He will persist in fashioning it into a vessel that is beautiful and useful. The heavenly shepherd will never abandon His sheep; He will make them lie down in green pastures and lead them beside still waters. His goodness and mercy will follow them all the days of their life. The vessel is safe in the potter's hand. The sheep are safe in the shepherd's arms.

Psalm 103

The Benefits of God's Grace

Psalm 103 is, undoubtedly, one of the best-loved psalms, just as Henry Francis Lyte's free paraphrase, "Praise my Soul, the King of heaven," is one of the most popular hymns in the English language. We have here the authentic utterance of a redeemed child of God, who piles up words to express his gratitude to the God of grace. His praise expands in three concentric circles. First, he addresses himself and seeks to arouse himself to the proper worship of God: *Praise the LORD, O my soul* (verses 1-5). Next, he recalls the mercy of God to all the people of His covenant (verses 6-18). Finally, he summons the whole of creation to join in the chorus of praise (verses 19-22).

God's benefits to me (verses 1-5)
The first five verses of the psalm are very personal, as the author confronts himself with his duty and exhorts his own sluggish soul to worship. He desires not only to praise God's *holy name* (verse 1), acknowledging the holiness or unique "otherness" of His being, but to remember *all his benefits*. Indeed, he is determined that his worship of God shall be as total as are God's blessings to him: *all my inmost being* in response to *all his benefits*. These benefits have been given to

Praise the LORD, O my soul;
  all my inmost being, praise his holy
    name.
Praise the LORD, O my soul,
  and forget not all his benefits.

He forgives all my sins
  and heals all my diseases;
he redeems my life from the pit
  and crowns me with love and
    compassion.
He satisfies my desires with good
    things,
  so that my youth is renewed like the
    eagle's.

The LORD works righteousness
  and justice for all the oppressed.

He made known his ways to Moses,
  his deeds to the people of Israel:
The LORD is compassionate and
    gracious,
  slow to anger, abounding in love.

⁹He will not always accuse,
  nor will he harbour his anger for ever;
¹⁰he does not treat us as our sins
    deserve
  or repay us according to our
    iniquities.
¹¹For as high as the heavens are above
    the earth,
  so great is his love for those who fear
    him;
¹²as far as the east is from the west,
  so far has he removed our
    transgressions from us.
¹³As a father has compassion on his
    children,
  so the LORD has compassion on
    those who fear him;
¹⁴for he knows how we are formed,
  he remembers that we are dust.
¹⁵As for man, his days are like grass,
  he flourishes like a flower of the field;
¹⁶the wind blows over it and it is gone,
  and its place remembers it no more.

¹⁷But from everlasting to everlasting
  the LORD's love is with those who
    fear him,
  and his righteousness with their
    children's children –
¹⁸with those who keep his covenant
  and remember to obey his precepts.

¹⁹The LORD has established his throne in
    heaven,
  and his kingdom rules over all.

²⁰Praise the LORD, you his angels,
  you mighty ones who do his bidding,
  who obey his word.
²¹Praise the LORD, all his heavenly hosts,
  you his servants who do his will.
²²Praise the LORD, all his works
  everywhere in his dominion.

Praise the LORD, O my soul.

both body and soul, for God both *forgives all my sins* and he[als]
all my diseases (verse 3). Further, He redeems my life *from t[he]
pit* (verse 4), that is the grave or Sheol. Not content with savi[ng]
the psalmist from sin, disease and death, God lavishes positi[ve]
blessings upon him as well. He *crowns* him (verse 4), that [is]
He makes His child a king (compare Psalm 8:5).

God also satisfies him *with good things* (verse 5), so that o[ur]
youth is renewed like the eagle's. Maybe this alludes to [the]
ancient fable that the eagle soars periodically so near to the s[un]
that it drops scorched into the sea and emerges miraculou[sly]
rejuvenated, or to the bird's annual molt and "eclipse" af[ter]
the breeding season, until the plumage is renewed the follo[w]
ing spring. Here, as in Isaiah 40:31, the eagle is used as a sy[m]
bol of youth and strength.

These, then, are God's personal benefits to the psalmi[st].
Delivered from sin, sickness, and death, he feels himself [as]
privileged as a king and as vigorous as an eagle.

God's mercy to His people (verses 6-18)
The psalmist now changes from the singular to the plural, fr[om]
the particular benefits which he has himself received to Go[d's]
general grace to all the people of His covenant. Whenever th[ey]
have been *oppressed* he has displayed on their behalf b[oth]
righteousness and justice (verse 6). The most signal revelati[on]
of this was to Moses and to the children of Israel under Mos[es']
leadership (verse 7). Such just dealing with His people was [an]
expression of His grace.

Indeed, what the psalmist goes on to write is a kind of me[di]
tation on that glorious revelation of God's name to Mos[es]:
"The LORD, the LORD, the compassionate and gracious G[od],
slow to anger, abounding in love and faithfulness" (Exod[us]
34:6). After quoting these words (verse 8), our author p[ro]
ceeds to enforce them by two negative statements, three illu[st]
rations and a striking contrast.

The two negatives indicate that God sets limits to his o[wn]
righteous wrath against sin. The first is a time limit, that [He]
will not always accuse. The second is a restraint upon t[he]
expression of His anger that, instead of that just judgment , [He]
does not treat us as our sins deserve (verses 9,10). Then foll[ow]
three positive illustrations of God's grace. His steadfast lov[e is]
as high as heaven, His forgiveness removes our sins as far aw[ay]
as infinity, and His pity is as tender as a father's for his ch[il]
dren, because He knows our human frailty (verses 11-14).

The mention of human weakness leads to the final underl[in]
ing of the mercy of God, which, as in Psalm 90, takes the fo[rm]
of a contrast between human transience and the eternity [of]
God's love. Humankind flourishes like grass, and perishes li[ke]
grass too when the hot desert wind blows upon it; but towa[rds]

Wild flowers beside the road, near Samaria. "As for man, his days are like grass, he flourishes like a flower of the field."

those who reverence God, keep His covenant and remember His commandments, His *love* and *righteousness* endure for ever and enrich their posterity (verses 15-18). This assurance of God's unfailing love to successive generations has brought comfort to many mourners as they have stood round the grave and watched a coffin lowered to its final resting place.

God's dominion over all creation (verses 19-22)
In the last paragraph the psalmist turns from the love of the Lord for His covenant people to His sovereignty over all His creation. He has *established his throne in heaven* and from there *rules over all* (verse 19). Thus convinced of God's universal kingdom, the author summons the whole created order to praise him. First, he addresses the mighty *angels*, called also God's *hosts* and *servants*, whose characteristic activity is to *do his will* (verses 20,21). Next he turns to the lower orders of God's creation and calls on *all his works everywhere* to worship Him. Finally, he comes back to himself and concludes the psalm as he began it, with the personal exhortation: *Praise the Lord, O my soul* (verse 22).

Psalm 104

The Works of God in Nature

Psalms 103 and 104 form a perfect pair and illustrate th
balance of the Bible. Both begin and end with the words *Prais
the LORD, O my soul.* Psalm 103 goes on to tell of the goodne
of God in salvation, Psalm 104 of the greatness of God in cr
ation (verse 1). Psalm 103 depicts God as the father with H
children, Psalm 104 as the Creator with His creatures. Psal
103 catalogues His *benefits* (verse 2), Psalm 104 His *worl*
(verses 13,24,31).

The author evidently has in mind the narrative of Genesis
and draws his inspiration from it. He follows approximate
the same order, beginning with light and ending with huma
beings. He describes with great poetic beauty how God mac
the heavens and the earth (verses 1-9), and provides drin
food and shelter for all birds and beasts (verses 10-23). Aft
a further meditation on God's many varied works in bot
creating and preserving "all creatures great and small" (vers
24-30), he concludes with a prayer that God's glory ma
endure, a resolve to worship God throughout his life, and
desire that sinners who spoil God's world shall be no mor
(verses 31-35).

It is important to notice the form which the psalmist
"gusto for nature", as C.S.Lewis called it, took. He does n
praise nature for its own sake; "there are no nature lyrics in th
psalms. Nature is referred to only to the extent that it points t
him who made everything" (C.S.Lewis). This emphasis is pr
served in Sir Robert Grant's fine (if free) paraphrase, "O Wo
ship the King" (1833).

God's creation of heaven and earth (verses 1-9)
Most of the verbs in this paragraph should probably be put i
the past tense and understood to refer to the creation of th
heavens (verses 1-4) and the earth (verses 5-9). We shoul
beware of taking these verses literally. The author writes as
poet, not as a scientist. We are not intended to picture God ri
ing on a chariot of clouds or building the earth like a house o
actual, material foundations. All this is imagery.

What the passage does teach us is that God is the creator c
the universe, and that He has revealed Himself in it. In H
essential being He is invisible, but He makes Himself known i
the visible order which He has made. The light is His garmen
the heavens are His tent, the sky His chambers, and the clouc

¹Praise the LORD, O my soul.

O LORD my God, you are very great;
  you are clothed with splendour and
   majesty.
²He wraps himself in light as with a
  garment;
he stretches out the heavens like a
  tent.
³ and lays the beams of his upper
  chambers on their waters.
He makes the clouds his chariot
  and rides on the wings of the wind.
⁴He makes winds his messengers,
  flames of fire his servants.

⁵He set the earth on its foundations;
  it can never be moved.
⁶You covered it with the deep as with a
  garment;
the waters stood above the
  mountains.
⁷But at your rebuke the waters fled,
  at the sound of your thunder they
   took to flight;
⁸they flowed over the mountains,
  they went down into the valleys,
  to the place you assigned for them.
⁹You set a boundary they cannot cross;
  never again will they cover the earth.

¹⁰He makes springs pour water into the
  ravines;
  it flows between the mountains.
¹¹They give water to all the beasts of the
  field;
  the wild donkeys quench their thirst.
¹²The birds of the air nest by the waters;
  they sing among the branches.

¹³He waters the mountains from his
  upper chambers;
  the earth is satisfied by the fruit of his
   work.
¹⁴He makes grass grow for the cattle,
  and plants for man to cultivate –
  bringing forth food from the earth:
¹⁵wine that gladdens the heart of man,
  oil to make his face shine,
  and bread that sustains his heart.
¹⁶The trees of the LORD are well watered,
  the cedars of Lebanon that he
   planted.
¹⁷There the birds make their nests;
  the stork has its home in the pine
   trees.
¹⁸The high mountains belong to the wild
  goats;
  the crags are a refuge for the coneys.

¹⁹The moon marks off the seasons,
  and the sun knows when to go down.
²⁰You bring darkness, it becomes night,
  and all the beasts of the forest prowl.
²¹The lions roar for their prey
  and seek their food from God.
²²The sun rises, and they steal away;
  they return and lie down in their
   dens.
²³Then man goes out to his work,
  to his labour until evening.

²⁴How many are your works, O LORD!
  In wisdom you made them all;
  the earth is full of your creatures.
²⁵There is the sea, vast and spacious,
  teeming with creatures beyond
   number –

living things both large and small.
²⁶There the ships go to and fro,
  and the leviathan, which you formed
   to frolic there.

²⁷These all look to you
  to give them their food at the proper
   time.
²⁸When you give it to them,
  they gather it up;
when you open your hand,
  they are satisfied with good things.
²⁹When you hide your face,
  they are terrified;
when you take away their breath,
  they die and return to the dust.
³⁰When you send your Spirit,
  they are created,
  and you renew the face of the earth.

³¹May the glory of the LORD endure for
  ever;
  may the LORD rejoice in his works.
³²He looks at the earth, and it trembles;
  he touches the mountains, and they
   smoke.

³³I will sing to the LORD all my life;
  I will sing praise to my God as long
   as I live.
³⁴May my meditation be pleasing to him,
  as I rejoice in the LORD.
³⁵But may sinners vanish from the earth
  and the wicked be no more.
Praise the LORD, O my soul.

Praise the LORD.

His chariot, while He makes the winds His messengers and fire and flame His servants (verses 2-4). "In comparing the light to a robe," comments the reformer John Calvin, "he signifies that, though God is invisible, yet his glory is manifest."

Similarly, the earth is described as having been established upon firm foundations and then covered with the deep. This is the primeval chaos, when "the earth was formless and empty" and "darkness was over the surface of the deep" (Genesis 1:2). Then the separation of earth from sea is dramatically portrayed (as in Genesis 1:9,10): the waters *flowed over the mountains, they went down into the valleys, to the place you assigned for them* (verse 8).

God's provision for birds and beasts (verses 10-23)
In this part of the psalm the verbs are mostly in the present tense, and remind us that Christians are not deists. The

nineteenth-century deists believed that God had wound up the universe and set it in motion like a gigantic clockwork toy. The Bible teaches, however, that God is a living God, ceaselessly active in the control and the care of what He has made. He makes provision for the *beasts of the field* and *the birds of the air* (verses 11,12). "Ecology" would be a term too grandiosely scientific to apply to this paragraph; yet this is what the author is depicting. He is fascinated by God's marvellous adaptation of the earth's resources to the needs of living creatures, and vice versa.

Thus, the streams which flow through the valleys provide drink for the animals (verses 10,11), while God's rain waters the mountains (verse 13) and the trees (verse 16). Similarly humans and beasts are supplied with food from the earth including wine, oil and bread (verses 14,15). Even carnivorous lions are said to seek their food from God (verse 21).

Living creatures require more than food and drink, however; they need shelter also, to protect them from the fury of the elements and in their breeding season. So birds, which *sing among the branches* (verse 12), also *make their nests in there* (verse 17). Storks build *in the pine trees* (verse 17), while *the high mountains* are a refuge *for the wild goats* and *the crags for the coneys* (verse 18; this is also translated badger and rabbit; it is evidently a hyrax). Further safety is provided by the cover of darkness, when *all the beasts of the forest prowl*. Then when *the sun rises... they steal away... and lie down in their dens*; whereas human beings, by contrast, work by day and sleep at night (verses 19-23).

God's creation and preservation of all creatures (verses 24-30)
The psalmist interrupts his descriptions with an outburst of praise (verse 24). Both earth and sea teem with His creatures *living things both large and small* (verse 25). The sea is also the place of ships and the playground of Leviathan (verse 26). The latter is evidently a great sea creature, which some scholars think "is the whale, some the porpoise; in Job 41 it is probably the crocodile". Whatever Leviathan is, God is represented in the Talmud as playing with it.

Further, if God has made all creatures in His wisdom, He also cares for them in His faithfulness. They *all look to you* (verse 27). They depend upon Him for their food and breath. Not that they are inactive in feeding themselves, for they have to *gather up* their food; but God *gives* it. This truth is further enforced by striking anthropomorphisms, which speak of God's *hand* and *face* (verses 28,29). Just as we have seen a child at the zoo or in the farmyard, offering food to some animal on the palm of an outstretched hand, so God opens His hand, that His creatures may be *satisfied with good things*. But when He turns away from them and hides His face, *they are terrified*. When further, He takes away their breath, *they die and return to the dust*. When, on the other hand, He sends His Spirit (or "breath"), they are not only created in the first place, but continuously renewed.

Food and life are the basic needs of every creature, and here their presence is attributed to the open hand and quickening breath of God, their absence to His hidden face. To modern ears it all sounds very naive. Can we believe such things in this age of science and technology? We have already noted that the descriptive passages are figurative, whether in the use of poetic or of anthropomorphic imagery.

But the truth behind the figures stands. God the Creator is lord of His creation. He has not abdicated His throne. He rules what He has made. No Christian can have a mechanistic view of nature. The universe is not a machine which operates by inflexible laws, nor has God made laws to which He is himself now a slave. The very term "natural laws" is only a convenient expression for the observed consistency of God's working. He is living and active in His universe, and we depend upon Him for our "life and breath and everything else" (Acts 17:25). It is right to thank Him not only for our creation, but for our preservation as well.

In conclusion, the psalmist expresses the fervent wish that God's glory (seen in His works) may always endure, and that God may continue to rejoice in His works, as He did when they left His hand at the beginning (verse 31; compare Genesis 1:31), lest He should look upon the earth with judgment instead of favor (verse 32). The psalmist determines himself to spend his whole life praising God and hopes that this psalm, his meditation upon the works of God, may please Him (verses 33,34). Yet he recognises that there are *sinners* and *wicked* people who do not give to God, their creator and preserver, the glory that is due to His name (verse 35). The God in whose hand their breath is, they have not honored (Daniel 5:23). His earnest desire is that such sinners should no longer be permitted to deface God's good world.

The city of Jerusalem from the Mount of Olives. Jewish pilgrims at festival time would have their first glimpse of the city when they reached the top of this hill.

Psalm 121

The Lord our Keeper

The fifteen psalms from 120 to 134 inclusive form a self-contained group. At one time they were probably a separate collection. Each is entitled *A Song of Ascents*, literally, "A Song of Goings-up." The most probable meaning of this term is that these psalms were sung by groups of pilgrims while they were "ascending" toward Jerusalem for one of the three major annual festivals. Each of these psalms, then, is a pilgrimage song. They are brief, and most of them show a great love for Zion and the Temple and an ardent desire for the peace and prosperity of Jerusalem. These little psalms all breathe a spirit of quiet, undaunted faith in Israel's God, *the Maker of heaven and earth* (Psalm 121:2; 124:7; 134:4).

¹I lift up my eyes to the hills –
  where does my help come from?
²My help comes from the LORD,
  the Maker of heaven and earth.

³He will not let your foot slip –
  he who watches over you will not
  slumber;

⁴indeed, he who watches over Israel
  will neither slumber nor sleep.

⁵The LORD watches over you –
  the LORD is your shade at your right
  hand;
⁶the sun will not harm you by day,
  nor the moon by night.

⁷The LORD will keep you from all harm –
  he will watch over your life;
⁸the LORD will watch over your coming
  and going
  both now and for evermore.

As they approached the hills surrounding Jerusalem, Psalm 121 would be an obviously suitable song for pilgrims to sing.

In the opening two verses the psalmist speaks in the first person singular, *I*. To his question in verse 1 about the source of his help comes his answer: *My help comes from the LORD, the Maker of heaven and earth* (verse 2). This sentence contains a remarkable combination of ideas, that Jehovah, the covenant God of Israel, is the creator of the universe. In verse 4 He is further described as the keeper of Israel, who neither slumbers nor sleeps. This, then, is the ground of the author's faith in God's ability to keep, namely the almighty power of the world's creator and the ceaseless vigilance of Israel's guardian.

Having talked to himself, the psalmist now addresses some fellow-pilgrim, and the rest of his song expresses variations on the theme of God's keeping power. Although our English translation conceals the fact by using the words *keep* and *watch over*, the same Hebrew word which they translate actually occurs six times (verses 3,4,5, twice in verse 7, verse 8). He who keeps the nation Israel is also the keeper of the individual Israelite (verses 4,5). He will keep him *from all harm,* watch over his *life* and his *coming and going... for evermore* (verses 7,8).

Psalm 122

The Peace of Jerusalem

This psalm is, more obviously than all the other "Songs o
Ascents," a song for pilgrims going up to Jerusalem for one o
the feasts.

The first verse expresses the thrill the psalmist felt when h
was invited to join the pilgrimage. By verse 2 he and the othe
pilgrims have arrived at their destination. Different thought
begin to crowd into his mind as he looks round about him. H
notices how *closely compacted* the city is (verse 3). He also
recalls God's purpose that the tribes should visit it for th
yearly festivals *according to the statute given to Israel*, refer
ring no doubt to the law recorded in Exodus 23:17. He remem
bers that Jerusalem is the centre of the nation's religious an
political life, where the people may either praise the Lord o
approach the *thrones for judgment*, if they have some disput
or law suit pending (verses 4,5).

After his meditation, the psalmist breaks out into a plea tha
people will pray for the peace of Jerusalem, and he gives then
a prayer to use (verses 6,7). Having asked others to pray, h
now prays himself. For the sake of his fellow-pilgrims and fo
the sake of the house of the LORD *our God* (which, above al
makes Jerusalem so precious), he will seek her *prosperit*
(verses 8,9).

¹I rejoiced with those who said to me,
  "Let us go to the house of the LORD."
²Our feet are standing
  in your gates, O Jerusalem.

³Jerusalem is built like a city
  that is closely compacted together.
⁴That is where the tribes go up,
  the tribes of the LORD,
to praise the name of the LORD
  according to the statue given to
    Israel.
⁵There the thrones for judgment stand,
  the thrones of the house of David.

⁶Pray for the peace of Jerusalem:
  "May those who love you be secure.
⁷May there be peace within your walls
  and security within your citadels."
⁸For the sake of my brothers and
    friends,
  I will say, "Peace be within you."
⁹For the sake of the house of the LORD
    our God,
  I will seek your prosperity.

The snow-capped peak of
Mount Hermon, in the far
north of Israel.

Psalm 123

The Uplifted Eyes of Faith

The background of this psalm is the scornful opposition of the
proud and the *arrogant* (verse 4). We can only guess to whom
the author is referring. It may have been any of Israel's
enemies. But it certainly fits Sanballat the Horonite, Tobiah
the Ammonite, and Geshem the Arab, who, when they heard
of the Jews' resolve to rebuild the city wall, derided and
despised them (see Nehemiah 2:19; 4:1-5).

The opening verses give a beautiful picture of quiet, patient
confidence in the God who is enthroned in heaven (verse 1). As
the servant's eyes look to the hand of his master, and the
maid's to her mistress's, *so our eyes look to the LORD our God*

(verse 2). This eye-to-hand gaze, as the analogy demands, expresses a waiting not for instructions but for provisions. It symbolises dependence, not obedience.

Having declared that he is patiently waiting for God's mercy, the psalmist now prays for it. His prayer is not an individual one; he identifies himself with the nation: *we have endured much ridicule from the proud.*

¹I lift up my eyes to you,
　　to you whose throne is in heaven.
²As the eyes of slaves look to the hand
　　of their master,
　　as the eyes of a maid look to the
　　hand of her mistress,
　so our eyes look to the LORD our God,
　　till he shows us his mercy.

³Have mercy on us, O LORD, have
　　mercy on us,
　　for we have endured much
　　contempt.
⁴We have endured much ridicule from
　　the proud,
　　much contempt from the arrogant.

Psalm 125

The Mountains round Mount Zion

Most of Palestine is mountainous terrain, and mountain
played an important part in the history of Israel. The pilgrim
approaching Jerusalem naturally sang about them (see als
Psalm 121:1).

Two mountain metaphors are combined. First, believers a
like Mount Zion itself, standing firm. Secondly, they are lik
Jerusalem encircled by mountains, for they are themselves su
rounded by the protection of Jehovah. Thus, God's people a
like a mountain surrounded by mountains, both immovab
and impregnable (verses 1,2).

The metaphors are now applied. God will not allow *th
sceptre of the wicked* (verse 3), which may refer to the mach
nations of the Persian-dominated Samaritans, to rule in th
land which He has *allotted to the righteous*, lest the righteou
use their hands to do evil. On the contrary, the psalmist pra
with confidence that God will *do good... to those who a
good*, but drive away the evildoers (verses 4,5).

¹Those who trust in the LORD are like
Mount Zion,
which cannot be shaken but
endures for ever.
²As the mountains surround Jerusalem.
so the LORD surrounds his people
both now and for evermore.

³The sceptre of the wicked will not
remain
over the land allotted to the
righteous,
for then the righteous might use
their hands to do evil.

⁴Do good, O LORD, to those who are
good,
to those who are upright in heart.
⁵But those who turn to crooked ways
the LORD will banish with the
evildoers.

Peace be upon Israel.

An orthodox rabbi leads a group of young Jewish children across the Temple square in front of the Western Wall, Jerusalem

Psalm 127

The Vanity of Unblessed Labor

It is useless to launch a new enterprise or attempt to guard old one, unless the Lord blesses these labors (verse 1). T house builder's labor is vain unless the Lord does the buildin and the city watchman's vigilance is vain unless the Lord do the watching. We may toil and overwork, getting up early an going to bed late, but all the time, if we only knew it, G *grants sleep to those he loves* (verse 2) or "gives to his belov in sleep" (Revised Standard Version). This, of course, is no condemnation of industry, any more than our Lord's teachi in Matthew 6:25-34 is a prohibition of prudent forethoug What is condemned is worry on the one hand, and feveri self-confident activity on the other. Both are symptoms unbelief.

Children must be recognised as *a heritage from the* LORD (verse 3), one of God's most precious gifts. *Sons born in one's youth are like arrows* (verse 4), for by the time their warrior father is aged they themselves will be old enough to defend and protect him. Moreover, if his *quiver is full of them*, he will be able to hold his own in any disputes *in the gate*, that is, in the space near the city gate where business is transacted and lawsuits are heard.

¹Unless the LORD builds the house,
   its builders labour in vain.
Unless the LORD watches over the
   city,
   the watchmen stand guard in vain.
²In vain you rise early
   and stay up late,
toiling for food to eat –
   for he grants sleep to those he
      loves.

³Sons are a heritage from the LORD,
   children a reward from him.
⁴Like arrows in the hands of a warrior
   are sons born in one's youth.
⁵Blessed is the man
   whose quiver is full of them.
They will not be put to shame
   when they contend with their
      enemies in the gate.

Psalm 130

Out of the Depths

The author's experience of forgiveness leads him to urge Isra
to trust God for redemption.

The psalmist depicts himself as floundering in deep wate
and *out of the depths* he appeals to God to rescue him (vers
1,2). These deep waters are a picture of his sin, guilt, and sen
of God's judgment – his own, and perhaps the nation's tc
with which he identifies himself (compare Nehemiah 1:4-
The author knows that if God *kept a record of sins*, takii
them into account and reckoning them up against him, neith
he nor anyone else *could stand* (verse 3). *But with you*,
immediately adds, *there is forgiveness* (verse 4).

It was this offer of forgiveness by grace without worl
which led Luther to call this penitential song one of t
"Pauline Psalms". Verse 4 was also one of the Scripture vers
which brought comfort to John Bunyan, author of *Pilgrim
Progress*, when he was convicted of sin. It contains a beautif
balance, because its first part brings assurance to the despa
ing, while its second part sounds a warning to the presumpt
ous. Far from encouraging sinners in their sins, God's forgiv
ness promotes that fear of the Lord, or reverent awe in His pi
sence, which leads men and women to depart from iniqu
(compare Proverbs 16:6).

Confident of the forgiving mercy of God to sinners, t
author now does two things. First, he affirms his own detern
nation to trust God for it. The ground of his faith is Goc
promise (verse 5). Thus assured, his soul *waits for the Lo*
(verse 6). His guilty conscience has brought him into the dar
ness, but he longs and waits expectantly for the dawn of Goc
pardoning grace. Secondly, he urges Israel to do the same. F
conviction regarding his own forgiveness (verse 4) leads him
affirm that *with the LORD is unfailing love* for Israel's sin
well (verse 7).

¹Out of the depths I cry to you, O LORD;
² O Lord, hear my voice.
Let your ears be attentive
to my cry for mercy.

³If you, O LORD, kept a record of sins,
O Lord, who could stand?
⁴But with you there is forgiveness;
therefore you are feared.

⁵I wait for the LORD, my soul waits,
and in his word I put my hope.
⁶My soul waits for the Lord
more than watchmen wait for the
morning,
more than watchmen wait for the
morning.

⁷O Israel, put your hope in the LORD,
for with the LORD is unfailing love
and with him is full redemption.
⁸He himself will redeem Israel
from all their sins.

Psalm 131

A Child-like Humility

These words, which paint the picture of a little child's contented dependence on its mother, seem to anticipate our Lord's insistence on the necessity of a child-like humility.

The psalmist contrasts what he is not with what he is. He is not haughty, he says, in either heart or looks. He does not occupy himself with *great matters* (verse 1). That is, he has renounced proud ambitions for prestige and power, whether for himself personally or for Israel after the Restoration, still humiliated under a foreign yoke. Instead, he is willing to be like a *weaned child*, no longer crying to be suckled, yet nestling contentedly at its mother's breast (verse 2). The condition thus pictorially described seems to be a person (or nation) who, weaned from arrogant ambitions, finds perfect satisfaction in God. It is a beautiful picture not only of humble faith but of what might be called the "motherhood" of God.

As in Psalm 130, the psalmist leaves his description of the lesson he has learned and urges Israel to learn it too. *O Israel, put your hope in the LORD both now and evermore* (verse 3).

¹My heart is not proud, O LORD,
   my eyes are not haughty;
   I do not concern myself with great
      matters
   or things too wonderful for me.
²But I have stilled and quieted my soul;
   like a weaned child with its mother,
   like a weaned child is my soul within
      me.

³O Israel, put your hope in the LORD
   both now and for evermore.

Opposite: An old Jewish
man studies the Scriptures
in the shadow of the
Western Wall, Jerusalem.

Psalm 133

Brothers Dwelling in Unity

The unity of the people of God has always been both His will
and the object of their desire. If this psalm is post-Exilic, it may
express the joy and solidarity of pilgrims gathered for worship
in Jerusalem, with the breach of the divided monarchy healed.

The covenant people of God are already *brothers*; but it is
both *good and pleasant* if, in addition to their fraternal
relationship, they *live together in unity* (verse 1). The pleasant
ness of unity is now vividly illustrated. It is like the consecrat
ing oil *running down on Aaron's beard* (from his head on
which it had been poured) and flowing down on to the *collar
of his robes*, and like *the dew of Hermon*, an expression for
heavy dew (verses 2,3).

We are not told why the unity of the people of God is like
Aaron's consecrating oil and Hermon's heavy dew. Some writ
ers have emphasised that both are said to descend, and that
their significance is the all-embracing influence of true
brotherly concord, sanctifying the whole body. At the same
time, since aromatic oil will have been used and the dew was
essential to the fertility of arid Palestine, these similes are
surely meant also to teach that unity is as fragrant as oil and as
refreshing as dew in Jerusalem. It is there that Jehovah *bestows
blessing, even life for evermore* (verse 3).

> ¹How good and pleasant it is
>   when brothers live together in unity!
> ²It is like precious oil poured on the
>   head,
>   running down on the beard,
> running down on Aaron's beard,
>   down upon the collar of his robes.
> ³It is as if the dew of Hermon
>   were falling on Mount Zion.
> For there the LORD bestows his
>   blessing,
>   even life for evermore.

Sunset over the Sea of Galilee. "Even the darkness will not be dark to you; the night will shine like the day, for the darkness is as light to you."

Psalm 139

The All-seeing Eye of God

This has been called "the crown of all psalms." It is certain a sublime exposition of one man's personal awareness of God's universal knowledge and presence. It is best known for verses 6 to 11, which unfold the impossibility of escape from God.

God's omniscience (verses 1-6)

The verbs paint a picture of God's perfect knowledge of humankind. He "searches," "knows," "perceives," "discerns," and is "familiar with" everything about us (verses 1-3). The divine knowledge extends to our thoughts, deeds, and words. First, God knows our thoughts *from afar* (verse 2). "Neither space nor time exist for God" (Bishop Perowne); all human thoughts are open before Him. Next, God perceives all *my ways*, including the activities of the day and the rest of the night (verses 2,3). Thirdly, God knows the words of our tongue, even before they are spoken (verse 4).

¹O Lᴏʀᴅ, you have searched me
 and you know me.
²You know when I sit and when I rise;
 you perceive my thoughts from afar.
³You discern my going out and my lying
 down;
 you are familiar with all my ways.
⁴Before a word is on my tongue
 you know it completely, O Lᴏʀᴅ.
⁵You hem me in, behind and before;
 you have laid your hand upon me.
⁶Such knowledge is too wonderful for
 me,
 too lofty for me to attain.
⁷Where can I go from your Spirit?
 Where can I flee from your
 presence?
⁸If I go up to the heavens, you are there;
 if I make my bed in the depths, you
 are there.
⁹If I rise on the wings of the dawn,
 if I settle on the far side of the sea,
¹⁰even there your hand will guide me,
 your right hand will hold me fast.

¹¹If I say, "Surely the darkness will hide
 me
 and the light become night around
 me,"
¹²even the darkness will not be dark to
 you;
 the night will shine like the day,
 for the darkness is as light to you.

¹³For you created my inmost being;
 you knit me together in my mother's
 womb.
¹⁴I praise you because I am fearfully and
 wonderfully made;
 your works are wonderful,
 I know that full well.
¹⁵My frame was not hidden from you
 when I was made in the secret place.
 When I was woven together in the
 depths of the earth,
¹⁶ your eyes say my unformed body.
 All the days ordained for me
 were written in your book
 before one of them came to be.

¹⁷How precious to me are your thoughts,
 O God!
 How vast is the sum of them!
¹⁸Were I to count them,
 they would outnumber the grains of
 sand.
 When I awake
 I am still with you.

¹⁹If only you would slay the wicked, O
 God!
 Away from me, you bloodthirsty
 men!
²⁰They speak of you with evil intent;
 your adversaries misuse your name.
²¹Do I not hate those who hate you, O
 Lᴏʀᴅ,
 and abhor those who rise up against
 you?
²²I have nothing but hatred for them;
 I count them my enemies.

²³Search me, O God, and know my heart;
 test me and know my anxious
 thoughts.
²⁴See if there is any offensive way in me,
 and lead me in the way everlasting.

In verse 5, the psalmist begins to anticipate the theme of the next paragraph and attributes God's knowledge of him to His constant presence both *behind and before*. He pictures himself as a beleaguered city. But this encompassing presence of God fills him with wonder, not fear, and he breaks out in praise of God's amazing, unattainable knowledge (verse 6).

God's omnipresence (verses 7-12)
This section begins with a question: *Where can I go from your Spirit?* (verse 7). It is important to observe, however, that this question expresses not the desire to escape, but the joyful astonishment that escape is impossible and that God's hand is everywhere to guide and hold him (verse 10). In order to emphasise the impossibility of escape from God, he mentions three conceivable escape routes or hiding places and declares that even there God is present. Thus, if he should ascend to heaven or descend to Sheol, the abode of the dead, God is there (verse 8). If he should *rise on the wings of the dawn*, a beautiful figure of speech for traveling at the speed of light, and reach *the far side of the sea*, even there too he would find God. No distance, from farthest east to farthest west, can separate him from God (verses (9,10). Next, if he should try to hide from God in the darkness, he would discover that God's eyes pierce through the gloom, since to God *darkness is as light* (verse 11,12).

God's omnipotence (verses 13-18)
God's omniscience, which in the previous section has been attributed to his omnipresence, is now attributed to His omnipotence. God can search man out not only because He sees him, but because He made him. The Creator knows His creatures through and through. The psalmist ascribes the wonderful development of the embryo in the womb to the creative power of God. Both his *inmost being* and his *frame* (verse 13,15) are God's. These together comprehend human beings, our body and our mind, emotions and will. The phrase *fearfully and wonderfully made* (verse 14), was originally suggested by the translator Miles Coverdale, but may be incorrect. Other modern translations render the phrase "for thou art fearful and wonderful." This wonderful creator-God while fashioning the writer, naturally saw his *unformed body* (verse 16). More than that, even before he was born, all the days of his life were planned and recorded in God's book (verses 15,16). Such divine knowledge and foreknowledge caused the psalmist to burst into praise. For the thoughts of God which he calls *precious and vast*, outnumber *the grains of sand* (verses 17,18).

He ends the paragraph with a statement whose meaning is

doubtful: *When I awake, I am still with you* (verse 18). Some writers suppose that he is referring again, as in the first two verses, to God's continuous presence with him whether he wakes or sleeps. Others think that he is referring to awaking from the sleep of death.

God's judgment (verses 19-24)

If only you would slay the wicked, O God! (verse 19). Many Christian readers feel that this sudden prayer sounds a jarring note after what has gone before. Yet it is perfectly consistent with it. When a person's world is full of God, they long for the elimination of evil. These evildoers are described both as *bloodthirsty* (verse 19) and as those who misuse God's name (verse 20), either taking His name in vain or exalting themselves against His authority. That is, they set themselves against both God and their fellows. In utter revolt against God's two great commandments to love Him and their neighbor, they do not even stop short of blood (violence, murder) or of blasphemy.

This, then, is the first point to notice. The psalmist is not expressing feelings of personal animosity or revenge. He has come to count God's enemies (verse 20) as his own enemies (verse 22). He is righteously indignant, where we would be unrighteously tolerant. He burns with a divine hatred of sin.

But, it may be said, this man failed to distinguish between evil and the evildoer. Should he (and we with him) not learn to love the sinner and hate the sin? Of course there is some truth in this. Yet it can be overpressed, for "evil" is not something abstract; it exists in the hearts and ways of evildoers. So when the judgment of God falls, it will fall upon evildoers, not upon evil in the abstract.

But, an objector may further ask, while hope remains we should surely desire not judgment of sinners, but their salvation? Yes indeed, but what if sinners refuse to repent? We cannot desire their salvation in defiance of their own willingness to receive it. This is the heart of the matter. The Bible teaches that the sinner is at one and the same time the object of God's love and wrath (compare John 3:16,36), and we should seek by grace at least to approximate our attitude to God's. We should earnestly desire the salvation of sinners if they will repent, and equally earnestly their (and indeed our own) destruction if they (or we) will not. It is because we find it difficult if not impossible to feel such sentiments, in divine purity without any admixture of personal venom, that we cannot easily echo the psalmist's words. But let us acknowledge the reason: it is because we know little of a truly righteous indignation .

Psalm 145

In Praise of God's Kingdom

The "kingdom" of God is the rule of God, both generally ove the universe and particularly over His people, and it is this tha is celebrated in Psalm 145. It is an acrostic psalm, each vers beginning with a different letter of the Hebrew alphabet i sequence, but its one theme is the glory and graciousness c Jehovah's rule. The praise which He deserves from His citizer is eternal and rational.

Eternal praise (verses 1-7)

The psalm opens with the author's resolve to exalt and prais God not only *every day* (verse 2) but *for ever and ever* (vers 1,2). Because the Lord is great, He is *most worthy of prais* (verse 3); since *no-one can fathom* His greatness, His prais must be unceasing. But no individual can worship God for eve on earth. So the author seems to be speaking as the representa tive of Israel and to be referring to future generations, each c which will declare God's work to the next and so perpetua His praise (verse 4). They will be occupied with *your wonde ful works, your awesome works, your great deeds* (verses 5-7

¹I will exalt you, my God the King;
   I will praise your name for ever and ever.
²Every day I will praise you
   and extol your name for ever and ever.

³Great is the LORD and most worthy of praise;
   his greatness no-one can fathom.
⁴One generation will commend your works to another;
   they will tell of your mighty acts.
⁵They will speak of the glorious splendour of your majesty,
   and I will meditate on your wonderful works.
⁶They will tell of the power of your awesome works,
   and I will proclaim your great deeds.
⁷They will celebrate your abundant goodness
   and joyfully sing of your righteousness.

⁸The LORD is gracious and compassionate,
   slow to anger and rich in love.
⁹The LORD is good to all;
   he has compassion on all he has made.
¹⁰All you have made will praise you, O LORD;
   your saints will extol you.
¹¹They will tell of the glory of your kingdom
   and speak of your might,
¹²so that all men may know of your mighty acts
   and the glorious splendour of your kingdom.
¹³Your kingdom is an everlasting kingdom,
   and your dominion endures through all generations.

The LORD is faithful to all his promises
   and loving towards all he has made.

¹⁴The LORD upholds all those who fall
   and lifts up all who are bowed down.
¹⁵The eyes of all look to you,
   and give them their food at the proper time.
¹⁶You open your hand
   and satisfy the desires of every living thing.
¹⁷The LORD is righteous in all his ways
   and loving towards all he has made.
¹⁸The LORD is near to all who call on him,
   to all who call on him in truth.
¹⁹He fulfils the desires of those who fear him;
   he hears their cry and saves them.
²⁰The LORD watches over all who love him,
   but all the wicked he will destroy.
²¹My mouth will speak in praise of the LORD.
   Let every creature praise his holy name for ever and ever.

Universal praise (verses 8-13)

The praise which is due to God is also universal, offered t
Him by all His creatures. This is only logical, because *he ha
compassion on all he has made* (verse 9). The glory that is give
by human beings to God is a response to the grace that is give
to them by God. And God gives grace because He is graciou.
Ultimately, both the eternity and the universality of worshi
arise from the gracious character of God. Verse 8 echoe
Jehovah's self-revelation to Moses recorded in Exodus 34:
and already quoted in Psalm 103:8. His nature of grace an
mercy expresses itself in universal goodness to humankin
(verse 9). Hence the universality of His praise. Human being
sing the glory, the power, and the eternity of His kingdom (ver
ses 11-13). The words anticipate the doxology at the end of th
Lord's Prayer: "Yours is the kingdom and the power and th
glory for ever. Amen" (Matthew 6:13).

Rational praise (verses 14-21)

The praise which is to ascend to God for all time and from a
people is intelligent worship, or what the Lord Jesus calle
"worship... in truth" (John 4:24). The only worship which
acceptable to God is offered in rational response to His revela
tion of Himself. That is, it is a worship of His *name* (verse
1,2,21), His eternal being as made known in His words an
works.

The psalmist now gives some concrete examples of God
gracious works. They show that His rule, though powerful,
not arbitrary. On the contrary, His kingdom is a beneficer
kingdom, and His throne a throne of grace. See how He cor
descends to succour His people in all their need. He uphol
the falling and raises the fallen (verse 14). He feeds the hungr
and satisfies *the desires of every living thing* (verses 15,16). H
comes close to those who call upon Him; He hears an
answers their prayers (verses 18,19). He protects those wh
love Him, but *will destroy* the wicked (verse 20).

It is noteworthy that in verses 19 and 20 God's people a
said both to *fear* and to *love* Him. One writer comments: "Fea
and love are the inseparable elements of true religion. Fear pre
serves love from degenerating into presumptuous familiarity
love prevents fear from becoming a servile and cringin
dread."

The last verse (verse 21) seems to summarise the thre
characteristics of the worship of Jehovah, which have bee
elaborated in the psalm. It is eternal (*for ever and ever*), unive.
sal (*every creature*), and rational (*praise his holy name*).

Psalm 150

The Final Doxology

The Psalter's doxology forms a fitting conclusion. As a summons to worship it is unsurpassed in grandeur. In common with the Hallel (Psalms 113-118) and the four preceding psalms (146-149), it begins and ends with the word Hallelujah or *Praise the* LORD. Further, every verse is an invitation to praise, telling us where and why, how and by whom, the praise of God should be expressed.

Where and why (verses 1,2)
Praise God in his sanctuary. The catalogue of musical instruments which follows clearly relates to Temple worship. But God is to be praised *in his mighty heavens* too (verse 1). So probably this verse is an invitation to both humans and angels to worship God – humans in earth's sanctuary, and angels in heaven. It reminds us that the praise of God is one, the church below joining "angels and archangels and all the company of heaven" in His worship.

The reasons why God is to be praised are found in His works and His nature, His doing and His being (verse 2). His *acts of power* are not specified, but will include His works of creation, preservation, providence, and redemption. They are the expression of His *surpassing greatness.* This is the perennial theme of worship – the greatness of God displayed in His works.

> ¹Praise the LORD.
>
> Praise God in his sanctuary;
>   praise him in his mighty heavens.
> ²Praise him for his acts of power;
>   praise him for his surpassing
>   greatness.
> ³Praise him with the sounding of the
>   trumpet,
>   praise him with the harp and lyre,
> ⁴praise him with tambourine and
>   dancing,
>   praise him with the strings and flute,
> ⁵praise him with the clash of cymbals,
>   praise him with resounding cymbals.
>
> ⁶Let everything that has breath praise
>   the LORD.
>
> Praise the LORD.

How and by whom (verses 3-6)

Every conceivable instrument is to be employed in the worship of Jehovah: wind, strings, and percussion (compare Psalm 81:1-3). The first is *the trumpet*, the ancient curved ram's horn. This is "the only musical instrument still in use in the synagogue", writes one commentator, "and the expert can make a prodigious noise with it." The other two instruments mentioned in verse 3 are stringed, *the harp and lyre*. Next come the *tambourine and dancing* (verse 4), and then *the strings and flute*, the latter being perhaps the simple shepherd's pipe. Verse 5 mentions two cymbals; the first possibly as small as castanets, the second larger and thus *resounding*.

So the orchestra is assembled. Worshipers are to blow the horn and pluck the harp, beat the drum, sweep the strings, play the flute, and clang the cymbals. "Noise, you may well say. Mere music is not enough... Let us have clashing cymbals, not only well tuned, but *loud*, and dances too," writes C.S.Lewis. What is here described is the uninhibited exuberance of lives devoted to God.

Nevertheless, the mere noise of instruments and movements of dancing are not acceptable to God, however beautiful, unless they express the devotion of our hearts and minds . The psalm's concluding verse (6), which calls on *everything that has breath* to praise God, may be intended to include the animal creation. Yet the emphasis is upon us human beings, the crown of God's creation, into whom He breathed the breath of life (Genesis 2:7). Our worship is not to be confined to church services. On the contrary, while we breathe, we praise.